THE 7 SUMMITS OF WINNING TEAMS

WHY SOME TEAMS MAKE IT TO THE TOP

JUDD EFINGER

The 7 Summits of Winning Teams: Why Some Teams Make It to the Top
Published by Upward Bound Media
Hailey, ID

ISBN: 979-8-218-04038-3
BUSINESS / Leadership

Cover and interior design by Victoria Wolf, wolfdesignandmarketing.com.
Copyright owned by Judd Efinger.
Author photo by craigwolfrom.com.

QUANTITY PURCHASES: Schools, companies, professional groups, clubs, and other organizations may qualify for special terms when ordering quantities of this title. For information, www.JuddEfinger.com.

Upward Bound Media

DEDICATION

THIS BOOK IS DEDICATED to the three most influential people in my life –
my grandmother, my mom, and my wife. It's no coincidence that they are all
women and shining examples of servant leaders.

My grandmother, Augusta, was the definition of class. She was an actress
and friend of Katharine Hepburn in Connecticut. She gave up her career
to raise a family of four daughters, and I am thankful for that sacrifice.
Grandmother demanded that all of her grandchildren acquire an education, be respectful, and have good manners. She also taught us to stand
up for what we believe. Before it was popular, she was an environmental
pioneer and figuratively stood much taller than her five-foot, petite frame.
Her greatest gifts were her service and commitment to her nine grandchildren. Unfortunately, she passed away in 1985 on her own terms. To this day,
all of my siblings and cousins and I firmly believe that each of us was her
favorite. What an incredible gift.

My mom, Susan/Suzy-Q, was a true saint and touched everyone she knew
in a special way. She also sacrificed a budding career to marry and become
a mother of four. I am thankful for that commitment and blessed to have
been raised by the best mom ever. My father chose to leave her and four kids,
all under seven years old, in 1968. Mom's response was to stuff all the kids,

our suitcases, and two cribs into a Peugeot station wagon and drive from Massachusetts to California to join her cause: Another Mother for Peace.

Life in Oakland during that time in history was a fantastic experience. We grew up very poor, yet I wouldn't trade it with anyone, because we had each other's love in abundance. My mom's greatest gift was her unconditional love and ability to make everyone feel special. She dedicated her life to her children and the Roman Catholic Church. Unfortunately, we lost her to throat cancer in 2011. She was my best friend and hero. I miss her dearly, and I know her spirit guides me every day.

My wife, Lisa, has taken over two pillars in my life as both my best friend and the best mother ever. She was an only child and lost her mom to kidney disease when she was only eleven years old. To her credit, this crushing event did not define her, instead it shaped her. She has dedicated her life to faith and family. We met at a small Christian college named Hope College in Holland, Michigan. We were both student-athletes, but admittedly, she owned the former and I the latter. Like my other two rock-star ladies, Lisa sacrificed a successful career as a stockbroker to stay at home and care for our three children. I couldn't be more thankful, and I know her mom is smiling down on her, full of pride. Lisa's greatest gift is her unconditional love and service above self. She has supported me every step of the way in all my adventures, and for that I will be forever grateful.

To my three brothers – Jay, Scott, and Kipp: I love you and am grateful to be on your team. And to my sister Kiki, whom we lost to a forty-year battle with heroin: Rest in peace.

To my three children – Kyler, Annekë, and Reinhold: I love you more than words can say and look forward to seeing your greatness shine as adults.

Lastly, to my collection of high school misfits that make up one of the best teams ever and a forty-year brotherhood – Dave, Eric, Mike, Paul, Ron, and Spence.

CONTENTS

ACKNOWLEDGMENTS

LIKE MOST MAJOR ACCOMPLISHMENTS, this book could not have happened without a winning team.

First, to the original pack of friends and adventurers who had the courage to join the vision of Wasatch Adventure Consultants at its inception (later rebranded as Park City Teamworks). Your contributions and those of countless world-class guides were essential to our success.

- Giff Brown
- Brian Brechwald
- Calvin Hebert
- Chad Linebaugh
- Bruce Matheson
- Patrick Ormond
- Caleb Van Sickle

Second, to our book research and editing team members who logged countless hours making this book a reality:

- Kimberley Labertew – We have worked together for more than fifteen years, and she brings one of the best business minds I know to this book. She was my essential listening board as well as the thought leader for three summits: Community, Creativity, and Courage.
- Annekë Efinger – She is our Millennial/Gen Y researcher and voice.
- Christian Labertew – He is our Gen Z researcher and voice.

And, finally, to our book team for making the dream a reality and for being so easy to work with;

- Polly Letofsky, Coach — My Word Publishing
- Patrice Rhoades-Baum, Editor — PatriceRB.com
- Victoria Wolf, Designer — Wolf Design and Marketing

Thank you all from the bottom of my heart.

What Are the 7 Summits of Winning Teams?

DURING THE 2002 WINTER OLYMPICS our small town of Park City, Utah, welcomed the world with open arms. The world responded by making it one of the most popular city and mountain destinations to visit, live, and play. Park City is now a significant destination for corporate meetings and retreats with more than a dozen world-class hotels within thirty minutes of the international airport.

In 1999, knowing the upcoming Winter Olympics would "put Park City on the map," I had the vision to leave a successful corporate career to start a corporate team-building and outdoor leadership company named Wasatch Adventure Consultants (later rebranded as Park City Teamworks). More than twenty years later, my bet on the post-Olympic springboard in Utah has paid off in spades.

This would also be a good time to state that I learned firsthand just how difficult it is to run a new business and avoid the graveyards full of new businesses that fail in the first year. It's hard work. We were certainly blessed with good timing, a great team, and the beautiful Wasatch Mountains. We are humbled and thankful to have worked with more than 500 companies and 40,000 business leaders.

This platform has given our team of facilitators the ability to witness how corporate teams play during outdoor adventures. We can hear the naysayers saying, "These team-building events are a waste of time and corny." Our answer: Like much of life, you will only get out of it what you are willing to put into it.

Our business adventures are designed to be real outdoor adventures with real business lessons woven into the experience. We simply let the business teams play the way they play. Under the stress of the adventures, we have seen it all. We will share some of our favorite stories in the following chapters.

We have had the privilege to work with some of the best companies around the world – from the leadership team of a small local ski resort to the worldwide sales force of a top tech firm in the *Fortune* 100.

It is important to note that more than 70 percent of the teams we have worked with have been sales and marketing teams, teams of high-potential or future leaders, and teams comprised of senior managers and executives. This may give our data some bias, but we truly have not seen very different behavior from the other 30 percent of teams from finance, engineering, and other groups. In fact, it may surprise you (or not!) that some of the most dysfunctional teams we have worked with are executive teams. More on that in the first chapter.

Additionally, we believe we have worked with more sales teams and senior leadership teams solely due to the fact that companies are traditionally willing to invest in more travel and training based on the perception of higher return on investment (ROI) for these employees.

THE 7 SUMMITS OF WINNING TEAMS

Winning teams are, have, or use:

CHIEF	=	Served by a 4S Leader
CHEMISTRY	=	Diversity of Thought and Complementary Skills
COMPASS	=	Common Purpose, Alignment, and Destination
CENTERED	=	Balance of Competition and Collaboration
COMMUNITY	=	Trust, Care, and Share
CREATIVITY	=	Solutions from Within
COURAGE	=	Overcome Adversity and Challenge the Status Quo

The list of 7 Summits of Winning Teams was born from our twenty years of working with business teams. We chose the word *summit* to represent a common pillar in our view of winning teams. We realize there is some overuse of the mountain metaphor, but it is a true passion for our team and a strong connection to the pillars of success – what it takes to be a winning team. We believe teams need to possess most of the seven summits to be on a path of success as a high-performing team.

If you are questioning where your team needs the most help, then I suggest you start with our 7 Summits Team Assessment. This will help you focus on your tallest summits first. In fact, I encourage you to take a few minutes to complete our Team Assessment right now. You'll find it in Appendix 1 and at www.ParkCityTeamworks.com. This assessment will shine a light on your strengths as the leader or team member. Conversely, you'll pinpoint specific areas of growth. This can give you a lens or perspective for deeper learning as you read this book.

It's important to note that we consider every professional to be a leader even if they do not hold a formal leadership role. The 7 Summits Team Assessment – and this book – offer useful insights and lessons that can help anyone become a better leader or team member and be part of a winning team.

A note on our research data – one of our core competencies as a team-building company is to end each of our adventures with a debrief and reflection. Each of our team guides takes notes and leads a discussion focused on lessons learned. We record the team notes over time and track common themes. These learnings became the 7 Summits.

When we created the list of 7 Summits of Winning Teams, we decided to present the Chief Summit first, because we believe a chief (strong leader) is the most essential pillar of a winning team. We are often asked, "Can you be part of a high-performing team with a poor leader?" Great question. The answer is that it depends on your timeline. Teams can win in the short term with a poor leader, but this rarely is sustainable over time. The research is clear: Strong leaders are the essential hub of the wheel for strong teams. The surest way to predict high performance from a team is to assign the team a strong leader.

In addition, we are excited about the Bonus Summit, because this chapter addresses the timely topic of post-pandemic hybrid teams. The global COVID-19 pandemic surely changed our lives and how we work, particularly since a great number of people continue to work remotely. Work teams may never operate the same.

We added two new team members from younger generations to help with our research. My daughter Annekë Efinger is a young woman carving out her place in the corporate world, and Christian Labertew is a recent university graduate entering the workforce. Together, they lent a fresh perspective to our view of surviving and thriving as a work team in the new, hybrid workplace.

We designed this book with a blend of storytelling and homework by presenting key takeaways in each summit's chapter, which you can bring to your workplace to make your team better. Since you made it this far into the Introduction, we assume you want to be on or lead a winning team. There is no better feeling than celebrating a successful summit win with your team back at the safety of Base Camp. Winning by yourself is cool, but sharing a win as a team is truly special.

Onward and upward,

Judd Efinger, Founder, Park City Teamworks

CHAPTER 1

CHIEF SUMMIT – The Winning Team Is Served by a 4S Leader

YEARS AGO AT PARK CITY TEAMWORKS, we began developing and honing the list of 7 Summits of Winning Teams. We specifically chose the word *chief,* because it started with the letter "C" and because of my affinity for the Native American culture. Dictionary definitions note that a chief is the leader or head of a group of people or an organization as well as the principal or most valuable part.

THE 7 SUMMITS OF WINNING TEAMS

Winning teams are, have, or use:

CHIEF	=	**Served by a 4S Leader**
CHEMISTRY	=	Diversity of Thought and Complementary Skills
COMPASS	=	Common Purpose, Alignment, and Destination
CENTERED	=	Balance of Competition and Collaboration
COMMUNITY	=	Trust, Care, and Share
CREATIVITY	=	Solutions from Within
COURAGE	=	Overcome Adversity and Challenge the Status Quo

One of my favorite scenes from one of my favorite movies, *Dances with Wolves*, is the scene from inside the teepee with the Sioux council. The council has gathered to discuss what to do with the white soldier they have captured (actor Kevin Costner). They are all sitting in a circle around a fire. The chief simply looks at each member of the team and allows them to speak on the subject. This process goes around the circle without any discussion, judgment, or counter point of view. The chief simply listens to everyone's position. He then says that it's not easy to know what to do, and the council should talk about this some more.

This is a very different leadership style than you would see in most rectangular boardrooms in business today – especially since the top executive leaders often express a strong opinion, which can bring a productive brainstorming discussion to a screeching halt.

The discussion format shown in that *Dances with Wolves* scene is known today as Quaker Dialogue (from the Quaker tradition). A key point is that everyone can comfortably share their comments without being interrupted or criticized. Quiet members of the team have just as much time to share their ideas as the more vocal members. Since only one person speaks at a time, this format promotes equal participation as well as thoughtful listening. It helps to gather around a circular table – instead of a rectangular table – to symbolically instill the sense of equality, with no one sitting at the head of the table. When everyone has spoken, the leader or facilitator summarizes the overall "sense of the group" or direction of the comments. We encourage you to try this discussion format – it could result in fresh ideas and new insights!

Another powerful reference for the strength of the circle in leadership comes from the legendary king of Britain, King Arthur. According to legend, King Arthur's successful reign was built on a circular leadership model – the Knights of the Round Table. The circular table was designed intentionally to have no hierarchy, so all members of the table had equal representation.

Over the years, we have encouraged business leaders to share this powerful symbol of strength by meeting in a circle.

We chose Chief/Leader as the first chapter of our book, because our experience shows that if you are looking for a high-performing team, then look at the top and you will find an excellent leader. Research backs this up.

An argument could be made that our team-building company data may be biased, because if a company leader has chosen to make a significant investment in management training, then they are likely either leaders who believe in people development or they work for a company that truly believes their people are their most important asset. While this may be true, we will also build a case for our premise that a winning team is led by a strong chief using published research on leadership.

Let's start with one of my personal favorites and one of the seminal business books ever written – *Good To Great: Why Some Companies Make the Leap and Others Don't* by Jim Collins. His research team set out to see if they could find any companies in the *Fortune* 500 that had been "good" and then made the sustained leap to "great." They identified seven companies that had made the leap to great, sustained it for more than fifteen years, and beat the general stock market with average returns greater than seven times. The short list of great companies includes such well-known names as Abbott, Fannie Mae, Gillette, Kroger, and Walgreens.

Collins then set out to find comparison companies in the same industries that had simply remained good. This allowed the researchers to analyze some of the common themes that separated the great from the good. The first thing they found in all seven great companies was a Level 5 Leader at the helm during and after the leap to greatness.

Collins presents five leadership levels:

- Level 5 Leader: Executive
- Level 4 Leader: Effective leader

- Level 3 Leader: Competent manager
- Level 2 Leader: Contributing team member
- Level 1 Leader: Highly capable individual

He defines a Level 5 Leader as someone whose personality blends humility and "professional will." It should be noted that these are not the characteristics of an autocratic, control-and-command leader. In fact, quite the opposite. These leaders give all the credit to the team and put the interests of the company before their own interests.

Our media often reserves front-page news for the big-ego leaders and CEOs, while the Level 5 Leaders are happy to stand in the background and lead great companies without the headlines. Good examples of Level 5 Leaders in today's business world would be Apple's CEO, Tim Cook, and Berkshire Hathaway's CEO, Warren Buffett. The best example that most folks can relate to in history is Abraham Lincoln. The sixteenth U.S. President never let his ego get in the way of the primary focus of leading his country through our darkest hours. All three examples are great chiefs, indeed.

A second piece of research, from the well-known Gallup organization, supports our premise that winning teams are led by highly effective leaders.

Gallup's 1999 book, *First, Break All the Rules: What the World's Greatest Managers Do Differently* by Marcus Buckingham and Curt Coffman, is a personal favorite and began my twenty-year journey down the path of learning about and teaching strength-based leadership. After interviewing thousands of the top 10 percent of the best-performing managers, Buckingham and Coffman found that the best managers shared these four common insights about leading the individuals on their team:

1. People don't change that much.
2. Don't waste time trying to put in what was left out.

3. Try to draw out what was left in (strengths).
4. That is hard enough.

We will take a closer look at strength-based leadership later in this chapter.

At Park City Teamworks, our own company research based on witnessing more than 500 team-building adventures with more than 2,500 teams shows that during the debrief sessions with the winning teams back at Base Camp, we found a highly functional leader (or leaders under a shared leadership model).

I entered the adult workforce in the mid-1980s, which was a wild time in American business with an enormous amount of wealth both gained and lost. The media was infatuated with CEOs such as Jack Welch, Lee Iacocca, and the early days of Bill Gates and Steve Jobs. What did they all have in common other than the obvious "pale and male"? They were all strong personalities who wanted to lead from the top with the spotlight brightly shining on them. We call this leadership style autocratic, control-and-command, and old school.

At that early stage of my career, I was infatuated with these leaders and wanted to learn as much as I could to model their success. For the past thirty years, my goal has been to read a minimum of twenty business books or biographies of successful leaders each year. These more than 600 books have helped to develop and mold my leadership principles. My first observation was that there is not one leadership model that works for everyone, all the time. Great leaders adapt their leadership style to each changing environment and changing team. Leadership is much more about art than science and is a skill that is honed by years of experience. With that said, leadership is an art that can be learned.

The modern worker is smart, diverse, and more socially responsible than any previous generation. If your company wants to attract top talent, then it must move beyond the old-school, control-and-command model.

In addition, your company must move away from "pale and male" leaders to a more diverse group of leaders. The U.S. Workplace Demographics table shows the stark lack of diversity in executive leadership in U.S. companies. It simply does not make sense that our top business leaders do not reflect the workforce they represent.

U.S. WORKPLACE DEMOGRAPHICS (2020)

Race	Population	Jobs	CEOs
White	60%	62%	93%
Hispanic	19%	17%	3%
African American	12%	13%	1%
Asian	6%	6%	2%
Native American	1%	1%	–
GENDER			
Male	49%	50%	85%
Female	51%	50%	15%

Compiled from HR data from Zippia – Diversity in the Workplace

The good news is that this table would have looked much worse ten years ago. Progress is being made slowly, and the younger generations are demanding change. The Zippia research is compelling – they found that more than two-thirds of job seekers think diversity in the workplace is a key factor when deciding where to work.

Let's keep peeling the onion. Why does the old-school, autocratic leadership model still prevail at many corporations and institutions? The answer is complex, but we will share our perspective.

First, it is human nature to resist change, and this is often even more prevalent at the executive level where hubris can create blind spots, which allow the status quo environment to remain in place. In public companies, the leaders may be forced to adapt to change as shareholders and the media demand that they better reflect the values of the modern workplace.

Second, resistance to change can be particularly true in private companies that do not have the oversight of public shareholders. In fact, family-owned companies often fall victim to the faults of nepotism and tradition. The older-generation board members carry the bias of hiring in their likeness, which extends the likelihood of doing things the way they have always been done. The best family-run businesses resist the status quo and evolve with each new generation.

Finally, the autocratic leadership model is very efficient, but notice that we didn't say *effective*, because that solely depends on the autocrat. It is an efficient model, because a single leader makes most decisions or an executive team typically comprises hand-chosen, like-minded thinkers. The single leader (or like-minded leaders) can make decisions quickly without the time extension of gaining group consensus. It must also be said that many employees enjoy being followers and being led by a strong leader.

We believe there are reasons to be optimistic about the future of leadership. Our hope and prediction is that the younger generations will demand change at the highest levels of growth companies. And those companies not willing to change and better represent the modern world will shrink their way into the shadows.

As students of leadership over the past thirty years, we feel there is a clear shift in the literature indicating that the qualities required to be a successful leader are changing. The Summary of Leadership Qualities table helps to show the shift.

SUMMARY OF LEADERSHIP QUALITIES

OLD-SCHOOL CONCEPTS		NEW-SCHOOL CONCEPTS	
Authors Published 1985-2000	**Leadership Qualities or Traits Emphasized**	**Authors Published 2001-2022**	**Leadership Qualities or Traits Emphasized**
Peter Drucker	Management by objectives Lead by example Productive meetings	**Jim Collins**	Personal humility Professional will
John C. Maxwell	Character Charisma Communication	**Patrick M. Lencioni**	Hungry Humble Smart
Stephen Covey	Inspire trust Clarify purpose Align systems Unleash talent	**Brene Brown**	Braving trust Embrace vulnerability
		Simon Sinek	Selflessness Empathy Grace Influence

It becomes clear in the business literature that we are witnessing a shift from the more traditional "hard skills" of management to the more modern "soft skills" of leadership. This is a positive sign that our leaders are becoming more representative of the modern workforce.

It makes sense that it will take time for the shift to become more widespread as the older, more traditional leaders age out of their positions and retire. We have witnessed the successes of the new, modern leadership style in the business adventures we have run in the last decade. These leaders are more open minded and less rigid. They are more flexible and willing to adapt their leadership style to both the changing needs of their people and the changing environment. We have named them 4S Leaders.

THE 4S LEADERSHIP MODEL

For years, we thought our company needed to develop its original platform for leadership. After reading hundreds of books and attending dozens of management training courses, I realized that few leadership concepts are genuinely original. This point is supported by the massive volume of more than 15,000 books that you can find in a quick Google search on leadership and management. The best models are thoughtful, simple, memorable, and time tested. We trust you will find that our 4S Leadership Model meets these criteria.

PARK CITY TEAMWORKS 4S LEADERSHIP MODEL

SERVANT:

- Begin with a strong heart and commitment to serve others.
- Use core values as the foundation for everything your team builds.
- Hire slow and fire fast based on values – zero exceptions.

SHARED:

- Have the self-confidence to share leadership with your capable teammates.
- Be the hub at the center of a strong wheel and always have everyone's back.

SITUATIONAL:

- Match strengths and experience to lead each situation.
- Adapt your leadership style to each unique situation.

STRENGTH-BASED:

- Build your team based on complementary strengths.
- Align your team's strengths with key roles and responsibilities.
- Set clear expectations and reward for performance.

The 4S's – Servant, Shared, Situational, and Strength-Based – are the foundational tools that the leader selects to be successful in any given circumstance.

The Native American medicine wheel has been used for thousands of years to represent the four directions of the compass and the four seasons. The strong image represents the circle of life and how the whole of the earth is connected. For our leadership model, the chief sits in the center as the hub of the wheel. Each of the 4S's represent one of the four spokes of the wheel.

4S LEADERSHIP MODEL

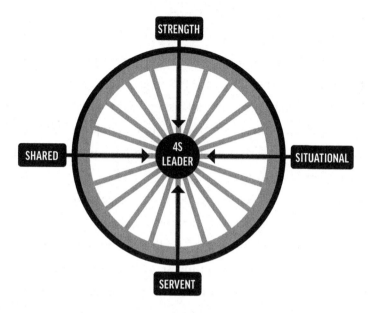

In the 4S Leadership Model a single chief runs the team. The team members report to one leader/manager who sets clear expectations and priorities. The chief remains accountable to the core results and team performance. Based on any given challenge, the chief may invite one of the team members to lead a project based on their specific experience or specific strength. The following paragraphs offer insight into our 4S Leadership Model.

CARABINER KEY POINT:

The key principle of the 4S Leadership Model is that the chief (leader) remains balanced and adapts their leadership style based on the given environment and personnel.

SERVANT LEADERSHIP IN THE 4S LEADERSHIP MODEL

The servant leadership model is popular in the modern business world. Even though the concept is thousands of years old, it wasn't until the seminal book *The Servant as Leader* by Robert K. Greenleaf (published in 1970) that this idea gained traction in the business world. The premise is simple – leaders have both the privilege and responsibility to serve their followers. Having been raised a Christian, one of the best examples of a servant leader is Jesus Christ. However, the servant trait is common with many of the great spiritual leaders of many world religions.

In business, servant companies put their people before profits, because as J. Willard Marriott of Marriott Hotels said: "Take care of associates, and they'll take care of your customers." Additional examples of servant leaders include Herb Kelleher at Southwest Airlines and Howard Schultz at Starbucks. Leadership expert Simon Sinek offers excellent examples of the power of serving; I recommend watching his YouTube video and reading his book, both titled *Leaders Eat Last*.

As it was taught to me in a management training session years ago, here is a solid acronym to teach the basic principles of servant leadership:

S – See the future.

E – Engage and develop others.

R – Reinvent continuously.

V – Value results and relationships.

E – Embody the values.

In our experience, you can find the servant leadership model being used most effectively at companies with strong values and core strengths that permeate throughout the organization. These companies do not shy away from their values, but they are proud of them. Value-based companies hire, promote, and fire based on their values. You can't miss a values-based company, because the values are proudly posted in the lobby and in every employee's cubical. (We will spend more time discussing values in Chapter 3: Compass Summit.)

A common misconception of servant leadership that I have heard while teaching seminars and leading team-building adventures is that service is a sign of weakness. Let's be clear – serving others is not a sign of weakness but of strength. In my career, I have received my greatest pride from serving others and encouraging their greatness from within to shine.

Service outside of work and in communities, schools, and churches has provided some of my most rewarding work. Our Park City Teamworks families have had the privilege to live and serve in Park City, Utah – a town that has earned the reputation of being a true community of service with over 100 nonprofits. I served as president of the Park City Sunrise Rotary Club and participated in many rewarding and meaningful projects for the benefit of the community. A shout-out to all the servant leaders in Rotary International worldwide who live by the Rotarian four-way test:

1. Is it the truth?
2. Is it fair to all concerned?
3. Will it build goodwill and better friendships?
4. Will it be beneficial to all concerned?

These are excellent questions to ask yourself and your team when making difficult decisions that may affect others.

Here is another question we are asked in our training sessions: "Are we born servant leaders, or can this be learned?" I believe all children are born of pure goodness and are ready to be molded into their own unique master-piece. Our parents, families, and "villages" mold us into who we are as adults. Gallup research shows that by the time we have grown into adult workers, we are mostly molded into who we currently are and who we are to become. Therefore, if we have grown up surrounded by givers, then we are far more likely to be committed to service as adults. And vice versa.

Author Adam Grant in his book, *Give and Take: A Revolutionary Approach to Success*, digs into the research to show that at work givers are more respected, more successful, and have larger networks than takers in the long run. Takers can win in the short term, but it is rarely sustainable. He notes that, for takers, success is a zero-sum game (a person can win something only by causing another person to lose it). On the other hand, givers find ways to "expand the pie" in ways that will benefit themselves and others.

So why aren't there more givers in the modern workplace? How have takers been able to build such a following? Good questions with difficult answers. Grant's research may provide one of the answers. His research shows that some givers landed in the group of top performers, while other givers landed in the group with the very lowest performers.

The important distinction between the two appears to be in how and why they gave. The low performers simply give for the sake of giving with no purpose. Not surprisingly, takers often take advantage of these givers. Givers who have a clear purpose in mind can still be givers – and can make a significant contribution to the organization – without allowing others to take advantage of them. The old saying that "nice people finish last" is only partially true, because they also finish first.

Can takers change and be converted to givers? Yes, but it is difficult to change as adults and overcome decades of bias. Consider this example: A young manager with success using an autocratic leadership style (taker) joins an established company with a history of servant leadership (givers). The executives want to bring in some new blood to run a new growth division and are attracted by the young manager's aggressive style.

Do you think the manager will adjust and learn a new and completely different style, or will the company adjust its proven style to the new manager? The answer is clear – neither will happen. This experiment is destined for failure, and the company should have screened out this managerial candidate during the interview process.

It should not be a surprise that givers become the best servant leaders. We should also be encouraged by the younger generations who collectively seem to have a bias toward service. Unlike those of us who began our careers in the "winner take all" 1980s, the young workers I see and read about today have a true passion for helping others, protecting our earth, and working for companies with a greater purpose. They are still driven to succeed, but they place higher value on service and purpose rather than just making money.

SHARED LEADERSHIP IN THE 4S LEADERSHIP MODEL

The next 4S attribute is Shared Leadership. This is much like it sounds, where the primary leadership roles are shared. It is a flat structure as opposed to a hierarchical, pyramid-like structure.

A personal example comes from the last executive leadership team I served on for a mid-size company in the water-management industry. The executive leadership team was made up of two co-presidents, a CFO, and two vice presidents. We each were responsible for the five functional areas of the organization. We all shared the same incentive program and had similar compensation. However, the co-presidents were also owners and sat on the board, which held us accountable to our commitments outlined in the yearly business plan. For the most part, we made decisions by majority rule with a common understanding that the two owners had our respect for the final decision. The five executives each led or sponsored key projects based on strengths and experience in the various functional areas of the business. Our team experienced years of successful growth using this shared leadership style.

Shared leadership is not very common in American business, because of our strong bias toward a more hierarchical organization chart. If the management articles in business journals are any indication, then the shared team and leadership models are certainly growing in popularity as the younger generations move into leadership roles.

Shared leadership can work well when there is a high level of trust on the team and an equal level of accountability. However, it can be a challenge to find a leadership team that has an equally high level of trust and performance among the members. If one spoke in the wheel becomes weak, the whole wheel becomes out of balance and eventually breaks.

Shared leadership can be rewarding and empowering, knowing you can make a difference. When the "wheel" is "in balance" shared leadership can be very efficient. The opposite is also true – it may not be empowering to report up to a single boss in a hierarchical structure, but it is quite efficient and keeps the accountability lines clean.

Trust will be a word you frequently hear when we talk about teams. I have heard it said and firmly believe that "trust is the currency of all humankind." It is the essential building block of all winning teams. Trust is elusive, yet you know when you have it and when you don't. Trust is fragile, because it often takes five good deeds to earn it, yet it only takes one bad deed to lose it. Heck, many teams we work with don't even want to talk about trust! We will take a deeper dive into trust in Chapter 5: Community Summit. If you want to lead or be part of a winning team, you must be comfortable trading with a trust currency.

SITUATIONAL LEADERSHIP IN THE 4S LEADERSHIP MODEL

The situational leadership concept was first named and introduced in 1970 by Ken Blanchard and Paul Hersey. They later developed slightly different versions of their model. Hersey wrote the introductory book, *The Situational Leader*, in 1985. Blanchard followed with his own book, *Leadership and the One Minute Manager*, in 1994.

The basic premise of the situational theory says that no one leadership style works best all the time. Instead, every unique management situation should dictate how leaders should manage their teams. A trained situational leader would then adapt the management style to a given situation.

The Hersey-Blanchard model identified the following styles:

- *Telling* – This leadership style is required when the team needs close supervision. Leaders may make all of the decisions and then communicate these decisions to the team. The team members may be entry-level with little or no experience. Following is required.
- *Selling* – This leadership style is typically used when a team or employee is stuck and not motivated to perform a task or job duty. Convincing is required.
- *Participating* – This leadership style is most commonly used when a team knows how to complete a particular task but lacks the confidence needed to complete the task. Coaching is required.
- *Delegating* – This leadership style is required when a team is both efficient and effective at a task. Little guidance is required.

In my experience, the situational model has some challenges in its purest form. Individuals and teams can be confused by the changing leadership styles. And leaders who are not polished practitioners may be perceived as too flexible and weak. This can be overcome with solid training and continued practice within the entire team.

At Park City Teamworks, the core principles that have always resonated with us are:

1. No single leadership style will work for every situation or team member.
2. Good leaders must first know themselves and know how to flex their style for any given situation.
3. Any given situation may require a unique set of strengths to find the best solution, so it should be matched to the appropriate leader for that given situation.

STRENGTH-BASED LEADERSHIP IN THE 4S LEADERSHIP MODEL

Strength-based leadership has most shaped me as a trainer and leader. I was first introduced to Marcus Buckingham at a *Fast Company* event in 1999. I was captivated by his passion for improving human behavior and his ability to communicate and connect with the audience. I was also impressed that he supported his presentation with mountains of Gallup research and data in his book, *First, Break All the Rules.*

The general concept of strength-based leadership made perfect sense to me for two reasons:

1. Employees want to do what they do best every day.
2. Intelligent workers would rather talk about what they do best than what they stink at. Not surprising.

The basic premise of strength-based leadership is that all adults have five core strengths that we have developed over time. If you can match those strengths to a given work task then work performance and employee engagement will increase.

While this might seem straightforward, Gallup research shows an eye-opening reality. After interviewing millions of employees and asking a simple question – "Do you use your strengths every day?" – the results were quite surprising. The following table published in 1999 shows the percent of employees saying "Yes":

U.S.	=	32 percent
China	=	14 percent
India	=	36 percent
U.K.	=	17 percent
Germany	=	26 percent

This research drove Gallup to launch a strength revolution over the past few decades. Let's begin by forming a better understanding by defining the term *strength*. Gallup defines a strength as "consistent near-perfect performance." Strengths are the combination of skills, knowledge, and talents:

- *Skills* are the how-to of a role. Skills are the performance steps that may be taught and learned.
- *Knowledge* involves the things that you are aware of and give you perspective. Knowledge is the combination of factual learning and experiential learning.
- *Talents* are the recurring patterns of thought or behavior that may be positively applied to performance. Talents are innate and often unique to an individual.

Discovering one's strengths is made available through a thirty-minute behavioral assessment named StrengthsFinder. Dr. Don Clifton developed this assessment more than fifty years ago, and it was refined by Gallup, which claims that more than 25 million people have taken the online assessment on its website. This strengths assessment is clearly validated by both time and volume.

Gallup has broken all human talents into thirty-four individual strengths that fall into four basic talent fields (see below). At Park City Teamworks, we have had good experience color-coding the StengthsFinder talents. We use the colors on nametags, bandanas, and elsewhere to help individuals easily remember their own talent and quickly recognize their teammates' talents.

1. *Striving talent (red)* – Fast paced, motivates others to action, focuses on excellence, likes a good battle
2. *Relating talent (blue)* – Even paced, open, trusting, people orientation, builds relationships, avoids confrontations
3. *Impacting talent (orange)* – Fast paced, passionate, driven, internally motivated, desires to stand out, competitive
4. *Thinking talent (green)* – Slower paced, linear, structured, practical, strategic thinking, weighs all the alternatives

I have taught StrengthsFinder over the past twenty years – it is a fantastic tool to identify an employee's strengths. I can only think of a handful of folks out of thousands of participants who have said, "This list of five strengths is clearly not me." I usually ask them to see if their spouse, other family members, or friends agree with the profile. Upon further review, even the resistors usually feel the tool does a very good job of identifying their core strengths. We will take a deeper dive into how to use StrengthsFinder as a tool to build great teams in Chapter 2: Chemistry Summit.

As a leader, the first step in using strengths as a tool to become a better leader is to take the assessment yourself. As Socrates said, "To know thyself is the beginning of wisdom." Paramount to strength-based leadership is to know your own strengths and tendencies as a leader. This will allow you to build a team around you with strengths that cover for your weaknesses, hence, increasing the collective strength of the team.

The next step is to "know thy people" by learning the strengths and talents of each of your team members. If you are just starting a new team, avoid the trap of hiring in your likeness. New managers often fall into this trap by hiring talent that is just like themselves, because they connect with the candidate during the interview process. This lack of diversity will lead to mediocrity as the team stumbles in the face of new challenges. Our experience shows that the best teams have a diversity of thought and strengths.

We encourage you to practice the 4S Leadership Model, because in our twenty years of witnessing business teams we've found that the best and highest performing teams almost always have a 4S Leader at the center. And when we ask these winning teams what makes their chiefs so special, they commonly answer that they are humble, smart, flexible, and caring. These are not adjectives we would have heard about great leaders from our grandparents' generation. Thankfully, our modern leaders are both representative and reflective of the more global, diverse, and thoughtful workforce.

INDOOR LESSON

Early in my career, I was asked to lead a team of forty sales representatives as the new vice president of sales for a mid-size, private company. The sales team had a long run of growth and success under the previous vice president of sales who was recently promoted to co-president. Tom's leadership style was hands-on, as he liked to be involved in all key decisions and had built most of the key customer relationships. As a solid, values-based company, the other co-president, Mark, spearheaded servant leadership as the companywide model and trained all middle managers.

As the new VP of sales, it was clear that this sales team had two significant challenges:

1. The team was aging and needed new talent.
2. There was no succession plan for key sales positions or key management positions.

I was committed to build on the past sales success while infusing the team with some new structure. As an example, the current structure had forty sales reps reporting to only three sales managers. Also, as a proponent of strength-based leadership, I knew I wanted to implement StrengthsFinder 2.0 for the entire sales team to provide the foundational data to begin a new, significant team-building process.

First step: I knew from experience that high-performing teams need strong leaders at the core and that the ideal team size for a single leader is five to seven team members. The math was simple: forty salespeople divided by the ideal team size of seven equals six leaders/sales managers required to run a healthy sales force comprised of six teams.

I started by getting recommendations from the leadership team on potential sales manager candidates – members of the existing sales team who showed leadership capabilities. We then overlapped all the strength profiles to ensure the team of six sales managers had complementary strengths and, at a minimum, carried all four StrengthsFinder profile themes: Striving, Relating, Impacting, and Thinking.

Second step: Hold an off-site workshop for the six new sales managers, which combined business planning with outdoor adventures. I chose one of my favorite adventure locations in beautiful Moab, Utah. The goals of the retreat were simple by design but challenging to execute.

I wanted to share the new strength-based leadership style, empower the team of sales managers to use their strengths, and collectively strategize activities for the five most important project milestones that the entire sales team needed to reach in order to meet our yearly business goals.

The new team of sales managers collaborated to identify the five key projects that would set up the sales team for success. In the off-site workshop, we listed the five projects and then discussed how to match the best strengths to each assignment and get some buy-in from the team regarding who would lead each project. As an example:

1. Design and deliver the first Customer Round Table = Relating theme
2. Identify new geographic expansion markets = Striving theme
3. Reassign customer-friendly part numbers = Impacting theme
4. Develop new profit-margin tracking reports = Thinking theme
5. Create modules for improved sales training = Striving theme

During the off-site workshop, I was happy to see the new team of sales managers work well together and self-select leaders for each project. I reassured the leaders that they were truly in charge of their respective projects, and I would assist the project team whenever needed as the executive sponsor for these projects.

The company had a process in which all significant projects required presenting a simple business case showing the ROI. As a 4S Leader I coached the sales leaders to present their business cases to the executive leadership team, knowing this was a good development opportunity for these professionals. I avoided the trap of simply taking all the hard work from these teams and taking all the credit in front of my peers.

We implemented our new strength-based model over the course of a few years, and it wasn't without its challenges. Change is never easy, but we stayed committed to my vision. Our sales team's performance was something we were proud of:

- We were identified as the top-rated team for employee engagement based on a companywide survey.
- We achieved the top sales revenue growth in the company's history.

- We increased gross profit margin and lowered the cost of sale.
- We led the company in the team/employee retention rate.

Indeed, this is an excellent business case that supports the 4S Leadership Model. Now let's look at some examples of 4S Leadership at work in a Park City Teamworks outdoor business adventure.

OUTDOOR LESSON

Our outdoor adventure example takes us to the meeting room at Stein Eriksen Lodge in Park City, Utah. It is a first-class hotel and ideal for business meetings and outdoor business adventures, because it sits adjacent to the slopes of the famous Deer Valley Resort. It's a spectacular autumn day with the alpine colors in full reveal. Today, our client is an international sales organization in the biotech industry, based in Salt Lake City.

This client asked us to present our Alpine Discovery activity. First, though, we like to begin our business adventures indoors, so participants can fully grasp the challenge and plan appropriately.

The first order of business is to explain the adventure in detail and ask participants to sign the consent form to participate. This is certainly part of the American legal culture, but it also elevates the participants' nerves, which is perfect because we want to see how they act when they are under some stress.

Next, we post the team list, so the group can organize at team tables and meet their new teammates. Prior to every adventure, we work closely with the company's HR director to ensure the small teams are thoughtfully selected to be cross-functional, from different locations, a good mix of genders, and most importantly, a blending of behavioral styles.

Once the teams have settled in, we introduce them to our guides/facilitators who are responsible for their safety and will observe their specific team's behavior during the adventure. The participants are traditionally anxious to hear the rules of engagement and quickly focus on how their team can win. We believe a well-designed business adventure balances the forces of team competition and company collaboration.

The Alpine Discovery event is our most popular business adventure. It's a high-energy adventure race. Teams start at Base Camp and must navigate to five camps where they must successfully complete each challenge to earn points – "revenue" – before racing back to Base Camp. (Some challenges have bonuses and penalties.) The team that earns the most gross profit is in position to win. However, in order for any single team to win the whole group must exceed the average corporate score for all Alpine Discovery events that teams have raced over time. This allows the teams to balance when to compete and when to collaborate. Just like at work.

We typically allow fifteen to twenty minutes for the teams to devise their plans of attack. On this day, we have five teams with six team members each. Our guides/facilitators try to answer safety questions but are encouraged to let the team dynamics unfold and let the team members play the way they want to play. We have found over our twenty years that teams often follow their normal *modus operandi* and reveal their true colors and company culture.

Here are the team notes straight from each facilitator's notebook:

- **Team #1** – "They started with my favorite questions: 'Has anyone done an adventure race before? Who is good with directions, maps, and GPS?' They keep asking me good questions even though I can't give too much information. There is no single leader. Beth asks who wants to be a communicator and then uses a walkie talkie. Beth keeps asking other teams if they can hear her. This is the last team to leave the room."
- **Team #2** – "We have a fun team. Positive attitudes, and they just want to enjoy the experience. They voted Jared as a leader – he was a Boy

Scout and hunter. Jared is a good leader and asks good questions. The team did not buy many resources, saying: 'We can find it if we need it.' This is the second team to leave Base Camp, and they have a solid strategy."

- **Team #3** – "The team seems stacked with triathletes. There is high energy, decent collaboration, and good discussion until they are interrupted by (I think) an executive named Bob. He suggested buying a lot of resources and filling their backpack with everything, because: 'We will need it, and we will be the best team anyway with the most points.' He stopped the planning and ordered the team to get going. No argument from the team. Here we go! First to leave Base Camp."

- **Team #4** – "Ouch, we have a know-it-all adventure racer as a dominating leader: Felipe. The team has conceded and is following his lead. He seems to have good ideas and is assigning roles based on experience. This is the third team to leave Base Camp."

- **Team #5** – "This team is super collaborative with three women. Casey seems to be a self-selected leader. She is a good communicator and is involving the entire team. Casey is trying to team up with Jared in Team #2 – it's kind of working. Sara is awesome on the walkie talkie and is talking to the other teams. She asked if anyone on the other teams wanted to share resources. Fourth team to leave Base Camp."

After reading the team notes, any guesses who won the adventure race? If you guessed Team #3 because it was stacked with triathletes, then you may be surprised to learn that this team came in last. Remember, this was the first team to leave Base Camp. Running fast in the wrong direction with no real plan is a failed strategy.

If you guessed Team #1 – the last team to leave Base Camp – then you were right. They won by a large margin of 11 percent more revenue (points) than the next closest team. The collective group did exceed the total revenue target and were saved by the collaboration and sharing of best practices by Teams #2, #4, and #5. Their good communication and sharing made a huge difference in the final results.

All Park City Teamworks adventures end at Base Camp with each team debriefing the lessons from the mountain and tying them back to lessons that can make them a better team at work. Let's spend some time reviewing how Team #1 practiced 4S Leadership by looking at excerpts from the facilitator's notebook and the team's debrief notes.

Alpine Discovery, adventure race rappel at
Kaaterskill Falls in Catskill Mountains

WINNING TEAM NOTES AND DEBRIEF

■ Situational and Strength-based – At Base Camp, Team #1 asked one of our favorite questions: "Has anyone done this before?" Lead based on experience not hierarchy.

- Shared – Right from the start of the planning they all agreed to share leadership, because they are all leading their own territories at work.

- Servant – At Camp 4 they sacrificed their tarp resource for Team #4. They were smart by calling all the other teams to see if they would need the tarp for any upcoming challenges.

- Strength and Servant – At Camp 7, which was a mind puzzle, a more vocal teammate asked the quieter teammate if she had any ideas, and she then helped to solve the puzzle. Introverts often have the best ideas and just need to be invited to participate.

- Situational – At Camp 1, which was a tent-building challenge, Team #1 began by asking if anyone had experience building a tent like this one and then quickly gave that person the leadership role for this task.

HOMEWORK/TEAM TALK

1. Begin by making a commitment to become a 4S Leader. Look in the mirror and ask yourself if you are willing to sacrifice the ME for the WE. If the honest answer is no, then stick with management and other task-driven roles. Leaders lead people. Managers lead tasks.

2. A key first step in your leadership journey will be knowing yourself. Use the behavioral assessment you feel most comfortable with and dive into the results. You can start with the 7 Summits Team Assessment in Appendix 1, which is also on our website at www. ParkCityTeamworks.com. Be open to accepting the results even if they show something you didn't expect.

3. Commit to being or becoming a servant leader by serving your followers and putting their interests first. Always have your team's back.

4. Be brave enough to make trust your team's currency. It is the foundation of all team building. Trust is both extremely valuable and fragile.

5. Be confident enough to share leadership within the team when appropriate and when the situation dictates it. Allow experience, not tenure, to dictate who leads and when.

6. Leadership is not static. Commit to being a lifelong student of leadership by improving and learning all you can every day. A minimum of one book or podcast per month is a good start.

CHAPTER 2

CHEMISTRY SUMMIT – Seek Diversity of Thought and Complementary Skills

A COMMON TRAIT we have witnessed from working with business teams over the years is that winning teams have strong chemistry. The concept of chemistry is challenging to define or capture. It is the glue that bonds all the elements of a team together. It's one of those things that you know when you have it – and you know when you don't.

THE 7 SUMMITS OF WINNING TEAMS

Winning teams are, have, or use:

CHIEF	=	Served by a 4S Leader
CHEMISTRY	=	**Diversity of Thought and Complementary Skills**
COMPASS	=	Common Purpose, Alignment, and Destination
CENTERED	=	Balance of Competition and Collaboration
COMMUNITY	=	Trust, Care, and Share
CREATIVITY	=	Solutions from Within
COURAGE	=	Overcome Adversity and Challenge the Status Quo

Dictionary definitions for chemistry mention the structure and properties of substances (you could replace *substances* for *people*) as well as a strong attraction between people.

In sociology, we have all heard the phrase that opposites attract. In physics, we know about the magnetic attraction found between two metals with the opposite charge. In team building, the best teams are balanced with a blend of different personalities and strengths. A team hired in the likeness of the leader with the same personality traits is destined for conflict and ultimate disappointment.

In their popular book, *Business Chemistry: Practical Magic for Crafting Powerful Work Relationships*, Kim Christfort and Suzanne Vickberg introduce a new tool to build work relationships. The two Deloitte Global colleagues began by studying what made the elite consultants stand apart from the average workers in a company of more than 100,000 employees. Interestingly, the star performers were simply more effective at building business relationships. And after further research, these outliers' secret sauce was *empathy*. The authors' definition of empathy: understanding and identifying with another person's perspective.

The word *perspective* is an important distinction, because it speaks to the ability to understand where someone is coming from or "walking a mile in their shoes." It makes sense that if you know where someone is coming from, then you have a better chance at a stronger relationship. It's the power of building bridges instead of fences.

The authors make a case for linking empathy and perspective to one's working style. They created a working style assessment named Business Chemistry. The tool is simple and memorable with four basic work styles: Pioneer, Integrator, Guardian, and Driver. We encourage you to learn more about the tool at https://BusinessChemistry.Deloitte.com.

The business world uses dozens of popular tools for behavioral and personality assessments. Like any tool, these assessments only work when they are being used and not sitting on a shelf. Park City Teamworks has used most of them, but we have focused on StrengthsFinder for its simplicity of understanding.

All personality assessment tools share the ability to create a common language for understanding within the team. While it might take a team five years to develop a solid understanding of each other, this can be taught in a two- or three-day workshop using a behavioral assessment tool. The lessons need to be practiced daily with your teammates, and then over time the insights become truly understood.

Regardless of your team's stage of development, we strongly recommend taking the StrengthsFinder assessment. In our experience, it is a great way to build a foundation for excellent team chemistry. This complex assessment works best when it is administered by a skilled consultant and the entire team participates.

As mentioned, we encourage you and your team to start on this path by taking the 7 Summits Team Assessment found in Appendix 1 and at www.ParkCityTeamworks.com. We have used this assessment with a great many teams over the years and have seen firsthand how it can enlighten and inspire individuals and the team as a whole.

However, your journey can begin right now with our quick and simple Park City Teamworks Strength-Based Talent Tool. We are introducing this simple tool here, developed by drawing from three well-known behavioral models: StrengthsFinder, DISC, and Business Chemistry.

Before we introduce our Talent Tool, let's look at where the three more complex assessments cross over and align in a combined table. Each column in this table is color-coded, which translates to our Strength-Based Talent Tool.

	RED TALENTS	ORANGE TALENTS	BLUE TALENTS	GREEN TALENTS
STRENGTHSFINDER	Striving	Impacting	Relating	Thinking
DISC	Dominance	Influencer	Steadiness	Conscientious
BUSINESS CHEMISTRY	Driver	Pioneer	Integrator	Guardian

The Park City Teamworks Strength-Based Talent Tool is a "quick-and-dirty" way to make an educated guess at your core strength – or a teammate's core strength – without having the benefit of taking a full assessment. It should not be considered a scientific alternative but instead a simple tool to offer some quick insights that can aid team chemistry.

We built our Talent Tool to be simple to use, experiential, and observation based. It is also important to know that people's core strengths come through more clearly during times of stress. Our brain's natural defense under stress is to default to our core strengths.

Let's start with the x-axis where we have Task on the left and People on the right. Under the stress of an important project at work, are you more likely to shut your door and dive into the details alone? Or are you more likely to call for a team meeting and get the opinion of others?

On the y-axis, we are looking at pace with Slow on the bottom and Fast on the top. Again, when things get busy at work and you are with your team, are you more apt to slow down and be more introverted? Or are you more likely to get energized and become more extroverted?

Now use the intersection of the axes to find the true median of your known work universe. Are you above/below or left/right of the center point? It is also important not to judge your guesses as there are no right or wrong answers. This really is just the start of some good introspection for you and good dialogue within your team.

PARK CITY TEAMWORKS STRENGTH-BASED TALENT TOOL

FAST

RED TALENTS	ORANGE TALENTS
Striving	Impacting
Dominance	Influencer
Driver	Pioneer
GREEN TALENTS	**BLUE TALENTS**
Thinking	Relating
Conscientious	Steadiness
Guardian	Integrator

SLOW   **TASK** ⟶ **PEOPLE**

As we wrap up our discussion on using behavioral assessments and work-style tools to build better team chemistry, it's important to know that this is hard work and typically takes time. It may be motivating to know we have witnessed that winning teams from the largest and most successful companies in the world have a blend of strengths and a diversity of thought. In short, they have great chemistry!

THE DYSFUNCTIONAL TEAM

It became clear to us after working with hundreds of corporate teams that you can't write a chapter about team chemistry without talking about dysfunctional teams or team members.

In their book, *Extreme Ownership: How U.S. Navy Seals Lead and Win*, Jocko Willink and Leif Babin name one of their chapters: "There Are No Bad Teams, Just Bad Leaders." We have certainly found that when you dig into the causes of poor teams, you will likely find a poorly performing leader. However, we have also found another common trait in dysfunctional teams: "There are no bad teams, just bad teammates."

We often get asked by business leaders to help them fix a poorly performing team. After a few team-building exercises and workshops, we commonly find a single dysfunctional teammate. The corporate world has many less-than-flattering names for these folks:

- Cancer
- Lone wolf
- Square peg in a round hole
- Toxic
- Misfit or mismatch

Clearly not names you would ever want to be called or words used to describe one of your teammates. In our experience, business teams often struggle to address these types of issues straight-on, so the problems are extended – or worse, they grow into larger team-performance issues.

CARABINER KEY POINT:

There are no bad teams, but there are bad teammates.

When we break down the dysfunction, we find it often falls into two "buckets":

1. **Bucket A: Human resources issue** – You simply made the wrong hiring decision, and the team member is not a good cultural fit or values match for the company or team. Action: Hire slow, and fire fast. Meet with your HR professional and map out a fair separation agreement. Always focus on maintaining dignity and respect. Note that your HR folks will ask you to document, document, document.

2. **Bucket B: Leadership issue** – The team has a performance problem that has not been addressed properly, and the leader needs to step up and find a solution. Action: Praise in public, and scold in private. These types of difficult performance discussions need to be open and thoughtfully prepared by both parties. They should never be a surprise if you desire a positive result.

The path forward for Bucket A (HR issue) is clear, yet helping a teammate move on is never easy. As leader, you will need to work closely with your HR people to resolve the issue.

We will walk through the details of a positive path forward for Bucket B (leadership issue), which both new and experienced leaders may find helpful.

To start, it is best to give your direct report twenty-four to forty-eight hours to prepare for his/her performance meeting. The leader should also frame the meeting with a minimum of three performance issues to discuss.

These can be issues brought up by teammates (never use names) or issues the leader has witnessed personally.

The meeting should be in person and in a neutral setting. Our strong bias is for a face-to-face meeting, but we understand that circumstances may dictate that the meeting be via video conference.

As the leader your job is to be well prepared with a series of good questions or statements that will drive a positive discussion. Here are a few examples that may be helpful:

- "I would like to address each of the performance issues separately, and I want to hear your side of the story, because your view is important to me."
- "You bring some unique strengths to our team such as _____. How can I help you use your strengths and blend them into the team to make us better?"
- "The way you have handled your disagreements is unacceptable and needs to change immediately. How can I help you find your voice in the team in a more constructive way?"
- "Do you believe in our team/company mission and goals? If not, how would you like to see them improved?"
- "Do you want to be part of this team? If not, how can I help you find a better match inside the company or outside the company?"

Again, these conversations are rarely easy, but it is essential to your team's health and your responsibility as the leader to find a solution as soon as possible. The goal should be to find a mutually beneficial outcome while being both firm and fair.

In these types of difficult performance conversations, there is no substitute for experience. If you happen to be a rookie, then it is best to ask for help from your supervisor or HR department. We wish you all the best in curing whatever is ailing your team and keeping you from reaching the top.

While team chemistry cannot be seen or touched, it's an incredibly important element in developing a winning team. In the previous chapter we gave an example of a top-performing sales team and how it was built with intention around strengths. The following story is a real example of building a winning team with complete strangers from around the world. Team chemistry played a big role in reaching the top.

OUTDOOR LESSON

In the summer of 2000, I signed up for an expedition to climb three summits in the Bolivian Andes mountains: Pequeno Alpamayo, Huayna Potosi, and Illimani. The peaks ranged from 17,600 to 21,100 feet in elevation.

I wanted to use this expedition to celebrate the life of a business associate and climbing friend, Stuart Matzke, whom we had lost unexpectedly. We had climbed a few peaks in the Cascades including Mount Rainier. Upon our return, we set the goal to climb a 20,000-foot peak in the year 2000. Unfortunately, in 1998 Stuart died of massive heart failure. The doctors believed his heart was weakened during his childhood battle with leukemia.

At his funeral, I signed the guest book with "See you at the top" and made the promise to honor the commitment we had made to summit a 20,000-foot peak in 2000. I got home and called the Leukemia & Lymphoma Society and filled out the paperwork for a pledge drive where friends, family, and work associates could help me raise money for every foot I successfully climbed in the Bolivian Andes.

After searching the Internet, I selected an adventure company in Salt Lake City named Camp 5. A few of its guides had successfully summited K2 (the second highest mountain on earth), which is far more recognized in the climbing community than Mount Everest. This company had a solid reputation for success in Bolivia and partnered with a local guide who had climbed Illimani in Bolivia more than 100 times. Early in my research I realized I would not be climbing with trusted friends, but instead I would be relying on strangers to screen more strangers to be my climbing partners.

This entered a significant element of risk into the equation. After much thought, I decided to ask to see the climbing resumes of the climbers who had been approved by Camp 5.

As I read the resumes, I had two thoughts:

1. The approved climbers all had solid climbing experience with Mount Rainier and Grand Teton as minimum qualifications.
2. This was an awesome opportunity to test some of my team-building skills. I had just founded Wasatch Adventure Consultants the previous summer (later rebranded as Park City Teamworks).

Camp 5 finalized the nine clients for the expedition and sent a thorough equipment list along with a six-month training schedule. Being competitive, I trained like a beast in the Wasatch backcountry that winter and hit most of the 12,000-foot peaks that spring and summer with a fifty-five-pound load in my backpack.

The nine climbers met at the La Paz, Bolivia, airport on July 7, 2000. We packed our expedition duffels on top of four decked-out Land Cruisers and set off to our hotel, excited to begin our climbing adventure.

The capital city of La Paz, Bolivia, rests at nearly 12,000 feet above sea level. Its elevation is more than twice that of Denver, Colorado, which is known as the Mile High City. Mount Illimani is in the background.

The team design for the expedition was to have three rope teams of four, each made up of three clients and one guide. We spent three days in La Paz, the capital of Bolivia, to acclimate and assess the strength of each team member.

Our head guide, Jose, had led many expeditions and knew the two most important things to a successful climb are fitness and teamwork. He told us our daily fitness hikes were to acclimatize and have fun, but we all knew we were being assessed and graded.

Interestingly, I held back to spend time with Jose and figured it was best to save energy. Plus, I liked being able to observe the others and begin to assess each individual's strength and the overall team chemistry.

Elizabeth, Tyler, and Mike's type-A personalities bonded quickly as they raced up the trails and were clearly very fit. Scott and Seth were in the second group and connected well as a Navy Seal and former Harvard hockey player – men's men. Annika and Charles were typically in the slower third group. They were both European and our elder team members. Charles was a "broken record" and talked the quiet and reserved woman's ears off. Chad was our super-fit mountain man and ran between the groups, checking in with all.

As we gathered for dinner prior to packing up for our trek up to Pequeno Alpamayo Base Camp, John, our manager, and Jose announced the three rope teams:

- Team 1: Elizabeth, Tyler, Scott, and guide Jose
- Team 2: Chad, Mike, Seth, and guide Rob
- Team 3: Annika, Charles, Judd, and guide John

My immediate reaction almost made me sick, as I was not comfortable with my life being in the hands of the weakest team. Jose did help by explaining that one of the keys to a successful rope team was that each team needed a strong anchor to secure the team in case of a fall. That would be my job.

Rope teams are typically made up of two to four climbers who are tethered together by rope and harnesses to travel across glaciers and snow fields. Each climber is also fitted with crampons and an ice axe to self-arrest in case of a fall or slide and help other team members as necessary. It is pure teamwork at the primal level – this was life-and-death stuff.

For obvious reasons I did not sleep well that night and realized I was pretty naive in my approach to hang at the back of the pack. However, I was beginning to learn a bunch about my expedition team. I decided my role was to help my team reach the summit. I self-selected my new role as Team 3 coach and cheerleader.

Pequeno Alpamayo's Base Camp was at a beautiful alpine lake at 15,200 feet above sea level. At dinner, we were told we would have one acclimatizing day for crevasse rescue training and ice-climbing technique and training. This seemed wise and another chance to assess skill levels. Most everyone performed fine with the exception of my teammate Charles. After bragging all day about his ice-climbing experience, he was a disaster nearly as soon as he put on his crampons. Another tough night's sleep for me.

Jose told us to set our alarms for 4:00 a.m., meet in the mess tent for tea, and be ready for a 5:00 a.m. start. Our goal was to summit Pequeno Alpamayo at 17,482 feet in elevation by 10:00 a.m.

Alpine mornings are truly special. I love the cold, squeaky sound of each step on the glacier and the focused eight-foot world created by your headlamp. As we clipped into our rope team, I felt anxious about being last as the other teams left. My teammate Annika was quiet, and I could tell she was all business. Charles was actually quiet for the first time in a week, and I could tell he was extremely nervous. I knew my job was to encourage him and elevate his confidence.

Enroute it was easy to see that our team was falling behind. Charles was a clumsy mess. I lightened the air by renaming him "Sir George" after the famous English alpinist George Mallory of Mount Everest lore. I also echoed the mantras of focus, breathe, one step at a time, and "pain is temporary, but glory lasts forever" (a quote from my high school track coach).

As we climbed higher on the mountain, I knew that if Charles fell this would endanger our entire team. I kept praying and tried to absorb the positive energy from the spectacular alpenglow of sunrise.

At our final rest stop in the saddle of the final spire, our guide John looked at me and asked how everyone was doing. I shook my head as we both looked toward Charles. John made the critical and right call to pull Charles off the rope team.

To his credit, Charles conceded willingly and asked what that meant for him. If one member of the team can't proceed and you are in a safe location on the mountain, then you "double-bag" the climber. We wrapped him in two sleeping bags and gave him a PowerBar and a Thermos of hot tea. We had an hour left of climbing and would return with a series of long rappels down the steep slope. Pulling Charles off the rope team was truly best for the good (and safety) of the whole team.

Our team carefully climbed the steep slope of the summit ridge and joined the other teams on top of Pequeno Alpamayo. The view from the top was spectacular. I thought about my family and my friend Stuart.

We descended, joined Charles at the saddle, and found him in good spirits. With clear weather, we made good time back to Base Camp and after a nice rest in our tents we joined a celebration over lunch.

That afternoon, I made my first journal notes with my assessment of each teammate's StrengthsFinder themes:

STRIVING	IMPACTING	RELATING	THINKING
Elizabeth	Seth	Charles	Annika
Tyler	Judd	Chad	Scott
Mike			

As a random expedition team, assembled over the Internet, we were actually a pretty good mix of personalities and talents. The Striving team members brought the drive for a result to the group. The two Impacting folks (including me) added energy and motivation. The Relating climbers gave the team a connection to each other, and the Thinking team members brought more strategy and detail to the group. All essential to a winning team.

Our next challenge was to blend the team's chemistry, so we could function at a higher level on the two higher peaks to come. Each night sitting around the campfire, Jose led a discussion about what we learned during the climb, and I added some team-building questions directed at how we could perform better in our three teams. After starting slowly, we had some valuable dialog and learnings.

As an aside, I believe there is great power gained from time spent around a campfire. In our business we have found that campfire discussions have helped many teams find their inner strength.

We broke camp and headed back to La Paz for a day, as it provided a central hub for all three mountains. We enjoyed a night out on the town as an expedition team and celebrated our first successful climb. Unexpectedly, at midnight, Charles announced that he would only be going to Base Camp for the next two peaks, as he was simply not up for the challenge. This was very unselfish and took courage. Silently, I knew it was best for the expedition.

The journey to Huayna Potosi took us past Lake Titicaca where we enjoyed a training hike and then camped for a night. The next day we endured a ten-mile trek up to Base Camp, but thankfully, this climb was fully supported by porters and llama packs. Base Camp sat at a nice meadow on the edge of a snowfield with beautiful views of the peak.

During dinner, Jose gave us the itinerary for the climb that included a night's stay at High Camp at 18,000 feet in elevation on the glacier. He also mentioned that his satellite weather feed was predicting storms moving in on summit day. I decided to hang with Elizabeth and Tyler during the climb to High Camp, because I was feeling strong and also wanted to make a bit of a statement – I was a capable climber completely up for this challenge.

Thankfully, all the tents at camp had been set up by Jose's guides, and you could hear the burners going for a hot supper. As we waited for the others to arrive, I explored the camp and stumbled into a makeshift graveyard for the eighteen or so climbers who had lost their lives on the mountain. I was taken aback by this and spent the next hour in my tent praying and trying to get my head back in the game.

We all found sleeping at 18,000 feet to be a futile exercise given the cold, anxiety, and headaches, so the primary focus was on proper body rest. The 4:00 a.m. alarm and a hot cup of cocoa could not have come soon enough. In the mess tent Jose announced his plan for the climb. Because a storm was moving in, he suggested we bypass the longer, normal route and take a shorter, steeper route straight up the south face. This route would be more physical and more dangerous, but it would save the needed three hours to beat the storm. He asked how the team felt about it, and after a few questions we all agreed to follow his advice.

We arrived at the headwall just after sunrise. The peak was lit in the classic alpenglow, and to me, this confirmed she gave us silent permission to climb. Jose asked Scott, Seth, and me to join him on the first rope team, so the big guys could kick steps up the deep snow and set pickets (aluminum poles to clip in the rope for protection). This was a good match for me as I had spent much of the winter in the Wasatch Mountain Range kicking steps during training climbs. Scott was a total beast and kept yelling the Marine mantra: "Nobody ever drowned in sweat!"

Once our fixed rope was set, the rest of the team could climb in our footsteps using an aid device called a jumar – it wraps around the rope with a handle and internal teeth, allowing climbers to pull their way up the rope.

Jose's plan worked flawlessly, and we summited Huayna Potosi at 19,994 feet – just ahead of the storm. The celebration was short, as we could see dark storm clouds coming and could feel a strong wind picking up. We rappelled the fixed lines as safely as possible and down-climbed past High Camp and all the way down to Base Camp. A long and physically exhausting day indeed.

The celebration was short that night. Everyone was spent, but we could all feel a higher level of team growth. We had met some adversity and fought through it together. The three *torros* (named by the local guides) had earned some respect by kicking in the steps for success. I was told it was a very stormy night, but I was sleeping like a log from exhaustion.

Our team was finally starting to gel with each team member beginning to respect each other's differences. Even the fast, aggressive, and somewhat selfish team members began to realize that we were stronger together than we were as individuals.

Our final peak, Illimani at 21,122 feet, is the second-tallest peak in Bolivia and stands proud above La Paz on clear days. During our briefing, Jose informed us that summit day would be much longer and would require us to sleep at High Camp before returning to the lower Base Camp. He also mentioned that the mountain is known as *cold mountain*, because you climb in its shadow for most of the climb, and it's always windy.

On the climb to High Camp I passed Jose and noticed he was struggling. I asked if he was ok. He replied, *"No bueno."* I made sure he drank some water, took his pack to lighten the burden, and encouraged him up the last thirty minutes to High Camp. He met with our doctor and rested in his tent. Later that night around the campfire, John told us that Jose was hypoxic (a low level of oxygen in his blood), and would be down-climbing to Base Camp with another guide in hopes of feeling better at the lower elevation.

Back in our tent, Seth and I were freaking out. Climbing Illimani without our head guide – who had climbed it more than 100 times – just didn't feel right. Again, I slept very little and prayed a bunch. Ultimately, we all decided to climb, which proved the strength of our team. Personally, I felt strong and was extremely focused to reach the summit for my friend Stuart as well as for all my friends and family members who had signed up to support this fundraising event for charity.

Jose was right about the cold. My thermometer read -23 degrees with a 40-mph wind. We were all anxious to get moving, so we could get the blood flowing. The cold mountain left a lasting impression on me. I was exposed to a minor case of frostbite on my right cheek. It remains permanently red, even twenty years later.

The summit climb was a sufferfest – cold, windy, long, and quiet. Quiet, because we were all bundled up, and the wind was deafening. I focused on one step at a time until our next scheduled five-minute rest stop every fifty-five minutes.

At just before 11:00 a.m. we finally made it to the summit ridge and the sunny side of the mountain. The wind on the ridge was likely 70 mph, but the warmth from the sun and warmth from being able to see the summit kept our pace strong.

Now only a few hundred yards from the summit, the most incredible thing happened – the wind suddenly died down and a silence overcame us. I truly felt like we were being touched by God. I became very emotional as we reached the summit and asked the others if they felt the same thing. Yes, they too were very emotional. I sat down to gather myself, pray, and say a final goodbye to my friend Stuart. *See you at the top.*

The author on the summit of Illimani.

All experienced alpinists know the work is only half done on the summit. Statistically, more climbing accidents happen on the descent. I knew my body was overworked, so I pounded some food and water and began to focus on a safe return down.

All eight team members reached the summit and made it safely back to Base Camp. We found Jose feeling much better physically, but he had not come to grips with the fact that he had let us down. We told him he had built this team to a high enough level that we were able to succeed on our own. The truth is that two of his strongest Bolivian guides had helped us overcome the adversity.

Upon our return to La Paz, we gathered for our celebration dinner, and our team was fairly subdued that evening. Maybe it was because we were all quite tired, or maybe it was simply the end of a long, emotional journey. Three weeks with perfect strangers on the edge of danger, and against all odds, we had built a special team chemistry.

On the plane flying back to the U.S. I felt conflicting emotions: guilt for leaving my young family and taking on such a selfish and risky adventure, sadness for leaving my new team of friends and knowing I would likely never see them again, happiness that I didn't disappoint my sponsors and raised more than $14,000 for leukemia research, and relief because I knew in my heart that this was my last big mountain climb. I would not pursue my goal to climb in the Himalayas. It was time to focus on climbing taller mountains like building a successful new business back home.

I also contemplated the lessons I learned from this experience, particularly those related to team chemistry. For example, having clarity on my personal strengths helped me to determine how I could best support my team. I assigned myself the role of Team 3 coach and cheerleader to encourage team members, keep up our energy and momentum, and ensure we achieved our goal. Being able to assess others team members' strengths also helped to gain insight into the team chemistry.

I often think of Charles as well. When he realized he was not up to the task, he made the difficult decision to step aside. A life lesson in the need for vulnerability in strong leaders.

Thinking back on our campfire talks, I realize it would have been easy for us to while away the time chatting about trivial matters. Instead, Jose and I purposefully used the power of the campfire to help us bond as a team, ask questions, and seek ideas to further strengthen the team. Leaders can take advantage of those rare moments when a team can talk honestly, be open to introspection, and be open to new ideas for improvement.

HOMEWORK/TEAM TALK

1. Commit to using a behavioral assessment for your entire team, so you have a common language to better understand and gain more respect for each other's differences and all that you have in common. You can start with the Park City Teamworks Strength-Based Talent Tool introduced in this chapter as well as the 7 Summits Team Assessment in Appendix 1.

2. Hire a consultant to successfully implement the assessment you choose, or work with an internal HR team member who is a Gallop-certified trainer for the StrengthsFinder assessment tool.

3. Build an Excel spreadsheet with the entire team's assessment profiles. We have had success assigning colors to the four key strength themes in StrengthsFinder:

    a. Striving = Red

    b. Relating = Blue

    c. Impacting = Orange

    d. Thinking = Green

4. Make strengths your team's common language to address conflict and tackle big challenges. Strengths should become the cornerstone of your new monthly performance reviews.

5. Hire an outdoor team-building company for your next retreat such as Park City Teamworks. This is the best way to see your teammates' true behavior under stress. Hint: Use the four theme colors in bandanas or nametags, so everyone can quickly identify their respective theme.

6. If outdoor activities are not a match for your company culture, then host dinner parties to get to know your employees outside the office. Be sure to spend some quality time with your team around a campfire, fire pit, or fireplace. It works!

7. If you are a new leader or taking over a new team, then get to know your team members by inviting them (and their family, if appropriate) out to dinner on the company's dime. Challenge yourself not to talk about work at dinner. It is a great way to break down the armor that most professionals bring to work.

You will know when your team chemistry is dialed in when you have one of the top-performing and engaged teams in your company, and you are the new model for 4S Leadership.

CHAPTER 3:

COMPASS SUMMIT – Ensure a Common Purpose, Alignment, and Destination

AS A YOUNG EXPLORER, Boy Scout, geology major, and adventure racer, I have learned to admire a good compass. According to Wikipedia the magnetic compass was invented in China during the Han dynasty in 206 BC. It was used for maritime navigation by 1111 AD. A common compass has a magnetic needle that orients itself to the earth's magnetic north.

THE 7 SUMMITS OF WINNING TEAMS

Winning teams are, have, or use:

CHIEF	=	Served by a 4S Leader
CHEMISTRY	=	Diversity of Thought and Complementary Skills
COMPASS	=	**Common Purpose, Alignment, and Destination**
CENTERED	=	Balance of Competition and Collaboration
COMMUNITY	=	Trust, Care, and Share
CREATIVITY	=	Solutions from Within
COURAGE	=	Overcome Adversity and Challenge the Status Quo

With proper training and maps, a compass is the essential tool to find your way home. It has also become a strong metaphor for life and business: Let your true north guide you. In their book, *True North: Discover Your Authentic Leadership*, Bill George and Peter Sims use the compass reference in the context of personal leadership. A key message is that your personal true north is your orienting point, which helps you stay on track as a leader. Your unique true north is your internal compass – derived from your deeply held beliefs and values – and it represents who you are at your deepest level.

This is a must-read book for any aspiring leader on the journey to find your life's purpose. And as we mentioned in the Chief Summit, a strong leader is paramount to winning teams. In this chapter on the Compass Summit, we focus on the team's common purpose, alignment, and destination.

First, let's explore the essential differences between a work group and a work team. I think this explanation will help to build a case for the importance of having a team compass. In his seminal work on business teams, Jon Katzenbach in *The Wisdom of Teams: Creating the High-Performance Organization* defines the differences. A team is a small number of people who are committed to a common purpose and hold themselves mutually accountable. In fact, the essence of the team is having a specific, common commitment. With no specific, common commitment, the larger work group performs as individuals.

Katzenbach nails the distinction between work groups and work teams. It remains my favorite definition of a work team. Yet, decades later, the word *team* is still one of the most widely overused and abused words in business. We often hear leaders say, "my team at work," yet with fifty-five coworkers they are likely a work group made up of many teams. The company may still have a broad set of collective goals, but it relies on many separate work teams with separate, more narrowly defined goals that all roll up to enable the company to meet its larger, strategic goals.

Also, many smaller groups wrongly call themselves teams. I have been part of and have inherited many sales groups that shared a common geography but did not have a common purpose. Instead, these sales groups were made up of individuals who were driven to reach their own sales goals and maximize their own sales commissions. This is not necessarily a bad thing for business, but by definition it is a work group and not a work team.

Let's look at how the first exploration to the South Pole shows the power of a winning team having a strong, common purpose and a shared direction on the team compass. The story is masterfully retold by author Jim Collins in *Great by Choice* by comparing the two strategies of the English and Norwegian expeditions.

In 1911, two teams set off with the goal of being the first to reach the South Pole. They both had the same purpose and exact compass headings: South Pole at 90°00'S / 0°00'E. Yet the fate of the two teams was drastically different. Let's explore why.

Robert Falcon Scott led the English expedition with an experienced Pole team, deep pockets, and all the most modern equipment. Roald Amundsen led the Norwegian team; it was poorly funded, had less Pole experience, and relied on traditional technology. The teams left within days of each other for a true race to be the first to set their country's flag at the South Pole.

Against the odds and most early predictions, Amundsen reached the South Pole first on December 14, 1911. Tragically, Scott's expedition ended in death, as they got caught in a storm before making it to their supply depot. Why did one team succeed and one fail, even though they had the exact same goal?

Collins's research revealed that the dichotomy in performance boiled down to two very different approaches in their planning, execution, and discipline.

Amundsen maintained a regimen of constant progress. He never pushed too far in good weather to ensure his team did not become exhausted, while he pressed ahead in poor weather to stay on pace. He actually "throttled back" his team to consistently travel about twenty miles a day, so everyone could rest and continually replenish their energy.

Meanwhile, Scott pushed his team to march up to forty-five miles a day when the weather was good and took full rest days when the weather was bad.

Collins links the 20 Mile March lesson to his research on the "great" companies that outperformed the market by ten times and concludes that "concrete, clear, intelligent, and rigorously pursued performance goals" will keep your team on track. When he compared companies with out-of-control, fast-paced environments to the "great" companies, he found that the "great" companies exemplified the 20 Mile March principle. They demonstrated an unwavering commitment to high performance in difficult conditions and the wisdom (and discomfort) of holding back in good conditions.

To be a winning team it is critical that you have a common purpose, and everyone shares the same destination on the compass. Equally important to your team's success is making sure you plan and execute with discipline, just like Amundsen.

At Park City Teamworks, our research from our business adventures supports this "slow and steady wins the race" philosophy. Only 9 percent of the teams that are the first team to race out of Base Camp actually became the winning team. When asked why they started the race in such a hurry, the most common answers were: "We wanted to be the first team to begin the race" and "Our plan was to figure out our plan on the way to our first camp."

The more thoughtful teams with the leadership and patience to develop a solid plan to clarify their purpose, alignment, and destination were most often the winning team. That is the power of the compass.

CARABINER KEY POINT:

Your team should never be in a hurry to begin a trek
before you establish and agree on your destination.

INDOOR LESSON

Early in my career, while leading a regional sales team for a water-management company, my boss asked me to accomplish two large challenges:

1. Turn a group of individuals into a team that shares the company's values.
2. Turn the region's profit and loss (P&L) statement to the positive.

As a seasoned sales manager, I knew how difficult the journey to building a true team was going to be. On one hand, you want a sales team that is passionate and driven to surpass their individual sales goals, and on the other hand you want them to see the benefits of sharing best practices to raise the performance level of the collective team.

The journey to building a team was introduced by psychologist Bruce Tuckman in his 1965 paper, "Developmental Sequence in Small Groups," and remains a classic. We will use his framework to help tell our story.

Tuckman summarized the five stages of team development as:

Stage 1: Forming – Establish ground rules.

Stage 2: Storming – Start to communicate feelings and resist control.

Stage 3: Norming – Team members realize they can achieve more together.

Stage 4: Performing – The team creates an open and trusting atmosphere.

Stage 5: Ending – Eventually most teams come to an end.

Forming – After being brought in to turn around a sales team that had been underperforming, it was clear that I needed to get the team together and establish the ground rules. The team was in its fifth year after opening a new manufacturing facility in California and had yet to turn a profit on the substantial investment. The top sales guy was outselling the other four sales reps by three times. Unfortunately, he knew it and acted like a true bully. Not surprising, this created an extremely competitive environment where the sales reps protected their own territories. This is fairly common in sales groups that are motivated by sales commissions.

The other significant challenge: The sales group had developed an adversarial relationship with the plant employees. The sales team complained: "If they could make the product cheaper then we could sell more." The plant employees complained: "If they could sell more then we could lower our costs by making longer runs." This is fairly common stuff in manufacturing organizations.

Storming – The year-end sales planning meeting would be different this year. I decided to move away from the traditional golf outing and, instead, hold the sales meeting at the plant. I told the sales reps we would begin our two-day meeting by building a few picnic tables for the plant group and cook them lunch as a thank you for all they did for our sales team.

I invited the plant manager to attend this two-day workshop and help with the sales forecast. This was a first. I also received permission from the president to share the regional financials with everyone. This level of transparency was also a first.

I started the meeting by writing a dollar amount on the board in red. I asked the sales reps if they knew what the number represented. Six tries and no one guessed it. The number was the dollar amount the company needed to become profitable. It was in red for a reason, because for the fifth straight year the regional operation had yet to turn a profit. It's helpful to know that the business case had predicted an ROI of less than five years. The room was silent.

The second piece of news was even more stark – we were not going to leave the meeting until we had concrete plans to lead the regional operating profit into the black and make a profit. We invited the CFO to join by conference call and agreed that we needed $X million in sales revenue (given the current profit margins) in the next fiscal year.

Our new common purpose – our compass direction – was $X million in revenue in the next fiscal year. Failure was not an option. It had taken the region five years to reach just 50 percent of that revenue goal, and now we needed to add the additional 50 percent in two short years. Game on!

Norming – The team's energy was fairly good as we prepared to end our meeting on the second day. The team members each stepped up with solid territory plans to reach our collective goal. It was obvious that the majority of the sales burden was on the top dog – the rainmaker. From Dave's body language I could tell this responsibility wasn't sitting well with him. I asked if we could share a ride to the airport once we had adjourned.

I asked how he thought the meeting went, and the reply was not that surprising: "The rest of the team is lame, and I get sick of always carrying the majority of the load." We talked about how being the rainmaker was not easy. It was a title that was earned with a bunch of hard work. I also told Dave he had the potential to be the best sales rep I had managed in my entire sales career. To his credit, he asked the right question: "What do I need to do to become the best?"

I replied that he needed to be a better teammate and share his good ideas and best practices. I told him this would make the rest of the team stronger and truly not cost him much in time or commissions. I asked him to think about this over the weekend and suggested that we could talk more when we were traveling together the next week.

We had a few good days traveling together and even found some common ground. At one point I asked him to name the three most important drivers that motivated him to work so hard. His answer was classic, "That's easy – money, money, and money." My quick-witted reply was, "In what order?" We both had a good laugh.

As we neared the end of our trip together, I told Dave that I didn't expect him to trust me after just a week of working together, but if he gave me a chance, we could help each other be very successful. In support of that comment, I offered him a sales commission "kicker" based on increased profitability. In short, he could double his commissions by increasing his profit margin and by helping his teammates become better.

Performing – The sales team had a magical two-year run in both sales revenue and operating profit. We expanded our team, added new territories, and surpassed our revenue goal. We also were proud to celebrate the fact that the California plant earned a well-deserved Plant of the Year award. Our sales team accomplished our challenging goal together as a true team. And we did it on the back of our rainmaker. Our success proved to be mutually beneficial. Dave helped to make his team better while becoming the highest paid sales rep in the company. I was fortunate to receive a promotion after the region became profitable.

Ending – All good things come to an end. This sales team remains one of the top-performing teams in the company, and Dave and I remain good friends. This personal business story represents a bunch of hard work and pride, but most importantly it highlights the power of the compass – working toward a common purpose with an unwavering commitment to reach the destination. It also shows the power of building a work group into a work team and converting the ME to WE.

OUTDOOR LESSON

In 1999, our budding adventure company earned our very first client, an international automotive company. We took the company's North American executives bobsledding at the Utah Olympic Park and began an ongoing relationship as its primary team-building company.

A few years later, they asked us to travel to Shanghai, China, and design an adventure race for the global leadership team. This group was made up of thirty high-potential leaders from around the world, and with 20,000 employees, these professionals were truly the cream of the crop.

We set off on our journey a week early to explore Shanghai and build a top-shelf experience for our client. We designed a course with eight stations located throughout the city as an *Amazing Race*-style competition. The small teams would compete against one another to meet a specific goal and win points at each station. We were fortunate to find a beautiful lake that rented dragon boats, and this became our water station.

If you're like me, you probably have never heard of dragon boats. They are truly unique to the Asian culture and provide an amazing team-building experience.

The boats we rented sat twelve team members with oars and in the stern, a large beating drum. Typically, we run teams with the ideal size of seven during our adventures. However, for this water station we thought it would be cool to ask two small teams to collaborate to fill the dragon boats, giving us a total of three boats with the thirty participants and a few facilitators (including me). This mix-and-match approach would force two teams to collaborate and communicate during a race that was primarily competitive. This clever design led to some clear learnings on the power of the compass.

The team I was facilitating arrived at the lake checkpoint with nearly perfect timing with a second team that we needed in order to complete this collaborative challenge. This required excellent communication from one of our teammates, Angie, who was a master of the walkie talkie and supported my claim that it is hard to overcommunicate.

As an aside, in our experience over the years, it is clear that women tend to be the best collaborators. I believe this bias may be driven by the ancient DNA built into women from both raising a family and the daily task of "gathering," whereas men may have a natural bias toward competition with a strong DNA built around competition, fighting, and hunting.

As the second team arrived at the beach launch, we read the station instructions and asked if anyone had any questions. Unfortunately, the two teams were still in a competitive state of mind and high on endorphins as they prepared to take the boat to the water. They took a pass on any questions, and sure enough the most jacked-up male started directing everyone to their seats. His brilliant instruction was to sit all of Team #1 on the left side of the boat and all of Team #2 on the right. He nominated himself to beat the drum.

Our dragon boat left shore in total disarray and with no true plan. Our self-elected leader was playing the drum like Alex Van Halen and yelling like rock singer David Lee Roth. After a few sharp lefts and rights, we nearly capsized the boat. For safety reasons, I stopped everyone's rowing and asked if anyone had a better idea on how to move this boat forward. We were truly two teams in one boat without a compass – there was no shared purpose or direction.

Much to my surprise, our team's most reserved introvert, Tien, quietly stated, "I have done this before and have participated in dragon boat races during recreation classes in high school." Brilliant! We finally had a leader with experience. She asked if anyone had any musical experience and could keep a double cadence on the drum. She then divided the rowing teams evenly based on people's size and weight.

She showed the entire team the large red buoy at the other end of the lake that we needed to navigate to and then return back to the beach, recalling this vital detail from the hastily read instructions at the water station's checkpoint. Finally, a common purpose, direction, and vision for the final target. She told the teammates on the left (port) side of the dragon boat to synchronize their paddle to the first low beat, and instructed the right (starboard) side teammates to paddle to the second high beat. She used the powerful beat of the drum as the central tool to give the team a common purpose.

It felt like Tien was dropped down into the dragon boat from heaven. Within a few moments of synchronized paddling, our group became one unified team with a compass. The experience was so powerful that the hair was standing up on my arms as our blue dragon boat cruised into the white sand of the beach.

Later, during the company debrief back at the lodge, we learned that our team had paddled the lake course a full twenty-five minutes faster, or 52 percent more efficiently, than the other two boats. A great example of finding the right situational leader, the power of the compass, and a team with a common purpose.

HOMEWORK/TEAM TALK

If you are leading a new team or struggling with group alignment and feel like you are wandering around in the wilderness of good or acceptable performance, then it is time to pull the group together and find your compass. Jim Collins was straight on when he coined the phrase "good is the enemy of great." Be the leader or team that accepts nothing but the best of everyone's full potential.

Here are some ideas to find your compass.

1. At your next off-site meeting, use the following framework to develop your team's compass. Draw a compass needle with a large triangle pointing north. Then draw a simple pyramid diagram with the following words:

GOALS

PURPOSE

VISION - FIVE YEARS

VALUES - SHOULD RARELY CHANGE

First, start at the base of the pyramid with values. This can be the collective company values, but this answers the question, "Who are you?" This statement should be at your core and rarely change. You should hire, promote, and fire based on values. Second, the team has to know "Where are we going?" – a vision of the future. This can also be the company's vision established by the executives or founder. Third – working our way up from the general to specific – is purpose. This answers the question, "Why do we do what we do?" This can also be called *mission*, but all teams must have an agreed-upon common purpose.

Fourth, get clarity on the daily, weekly, monthly, and quarterly common goals that the team will use to hold each other accountable. The goals answer the question: "How do we get there?" It's the piece that represents the compass needle.

2. Now that you have developed your compass, it's important to refine it and test it with your team each month or quarter. If each team member can't recite your common purpose – essentially your 20 Mile March – then it needs more work.

3. It is also critical that your new team compass aligns with the common direction of the collective organization. Share it with your leaders and make sure you have alignment.

When you have everyone on your boat rowing in the same direction toward the same destination, it is the best feeling in the world.

CHAPTER 4:

CENTERED SUMMIT – Balance Competition and Collaboration

MY MOM SPENT MUCH OF HER LIFE in New England like the poet Robert Frost. She learned to respect the changing seasons and the dichotomy of life. The harshness of the bitter-cold winters balanced with the warm, humid summers. Yet, for many New Englanders, you learn to cherish the two seasons in between – fall and spring – for the balance of it all.

My mom loved this poem by Robert Frost: "We dance round in a ring and suppose, But the secret sits in the middle and knows." What is Frost trying to say in this short verse? In my mom's view, we spend too much of our youth trying to find greatness on the fringes of life, and as we age and become wiser, we learn that the answers to life often are found in the center. The wiser I get, the more I concur – the answers often sit in the middle.

THE 7 SUMMITS OF WINNING TEAMS
Winning teams are, have, or use:

CHIEF	=	Served by a 4S Leader
CHEMISTRY	=	Diversity of Thought and Complementary Skills
COMPASS	=	Common Purpose, Alignment, and Destination
CENTERED	=	**Balance of Competition and Collaboration**
COMMUNITY	=	Trust, Care, and Share
CREATIVITY	=	Solutions from Within
COURAGE	=	Overcome Adversity and Challenge the Status Quo

Our research shows that winning teams are "centered" with a balance of competition and collaboration. They dance in the middle third of the spectrum and flex to be more collaborative or more competitive given the appropriate situation.

COLLABORATION ←——— WINNING TEAMS ———→ COMPETITION

This dance in the middle – a healthy balance of collaboration and competition – is more art than science. It requires solid leadership and an experienced team open to being flexible to adapt to their environment. Let's talk about the two extremes first, so we can better understand the outer boundaries.

COMPETITION/SCARCITY
Most of my family, friends, and foe would likely call me highly competitive. In fact, I hate to lose in almost anything. Admittedly, as a young adult I lived out of balance and weighted my behavior and actions toward competition. However, over the years, I have moved toward the middle by seeing the power of collaboration.

Other than experience and wisdom, what helped to change me? The answer is simple – marriage and children. Marriage because my wife taught me to chill out and, through mutual respect, we have become a powerful partnership. Children because during the miracle of birth, a man becomes a father and evolves into being part of the very best team of all – *mi familia*.

The United States was founded on freedom and built on capitalism. America has flourished under competition. However, the modern, global economy is demanding change in order to be successful. The new world order is moving more toward the middle, and success will require more collaboration.

High competition is rooted in a scarcity mindset. A scarcity thinker believes the business world is made up of a limited number of resources, and we all compete for those finite resources. Using the pie metaphor, we are limited to one pie, and each of us must compete for the largest piece of the pie. The clear goal in the scarcity mindset is to win the resources, and if you win then your competitor loses. This can be defined as win-loss, a concept made popular in the book *The 7 Habits of Highly Effective People* by Stephen R. Covey.

A win-loss, scarcity mentality drives us to be threatened by others, so we compete for a limited outcome rather than working together to achieve a much bigger outcome. Supporters of the competitive model will say that the name of the game in business is winning at any cost. And in the history of capitalism, there are countless examples of successful, competitively driven companies. However, the opposite is also true: There are countless examples of competitive companies that ended up on the long list of going bankrupt.

COLLABORATION/ABUNDANCE

The opposite of scarcity is abundance. In the abundant mindset there is a shift away from competition and toward collaboration. An abundant thinker believes the world has solutions to all the limiting problems. Instead of finding ways to gain a larger piece of pie, we will find a way to make more pies.

The twenty-first century has provided an amazing opportunity for abundance through technology, which can assure abundance for all. In their book, *Abundance: The Future Is Better Than You Think*, Peter H. Diamandis and Steven Kotler make a strong case for how technology is transforming our world. A key point is that technology has the potential to significantly raise the basic standard of living for every person on earth. Goods and services that were once reserved for the wealthy few can be provided to anyone who needs them.

In the Covey model, an abundant thinker always looks for a win-win solution. If you come from a belief that there truly is enough for everyone, then you naturally look for solutions that are mutually beneficial. When teams work together to find solutions, the outcomes can grow exponentially.

Supporters of the collaboration model will say that there is no downside to being a sharing team or company. We would argue that business teams can, in fact, be overly collaborative, as shown in one of the Outdoor Lessons in the following pages. The reality is that both time and resources within a company are limited, so if you are spending too much time or money helping other teams, then your team may be out of balance. Sharing time and money to collaborate is often a wise investment knowing it will be repaid in the future. However, if the collaboration is keeping you from attaining your own team goals or is a distraction from your focus, then it may be totally fine to delay the request for a later time.

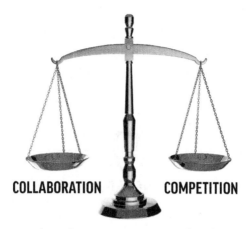

COLLABORATION   COMPETITION

Your team's goal is to remain centered with an equal
balance of collaboration and competition.

CENTERED

The concept of being centered is represented by the scale diagram. The goal for a centered team is to operate with proper balance in the middle area between collaboration and competition. The team's goal is to operate in balance, so neither side of the scale drops low enough to touch the base.

A well-centered team flexes their weight toward one end or the other based on the environment but always stays in balance. This is the sweet spot for top performance. How does a team know when they are centered and, more importantly, when they are out of balance? Like many things, it is an awareness that comes from experience – both good and bad. Later in this chapter you will read some lessons that will help your team find their balance.

First and foremost, build your team with a balance of strengths and a diversity of thought as we discussed in the Chemistry Summit. In StrengthsFinder language, for every driven, competitive Striver on your team you should have a collaborative Thinker or Relator. For every introvert you should bring in the balance of an extrovert.

In my experience, a balanced team will know how to find their center by respecting each other's point of view and then having the courage to push back when they see the team is too far on the edges. While it can be challenging, you and your team should strive to continually find the balance between collaboration and competition.

CARABINER KEY POINT:

Compete outside your organization.
Collaborate inside your organization.

WHEN TO COMPETE AND WHEN TO COLLABORATE

A key takeaway for this Centered Summit is to compete aggressively *outside* your organization and collaborate enthusiastically *inside* your organization.

This seems quite simple, but our experience in working with hundreds of companies is that far too often teams compete for resources and attention with other teams within their own company. When we ask company leaders why this is we often hear shallow answers like, "It's part of our culture to be competitive" or "We're working to remove the silos between departments."

Let's break down these statements. If your company has a strong competitive culture, then you should never get rid of it. Instead, find a way to redirect it externally to your competitors. It is healthy capitalism to have a strong desire to beat the competition and win the business. However, that strong competitive energy should never be used to beat someone or another team within your organization. It just doesn't make sense to keep supporting and rewarding teams that create win-lose scenarios within the company when you are all trying to meet the same strategic goals.

The term *silo* has become part of the corporate vernacular as a symbol for separate and individual functional areas within a company. These functional and geographic silos naturally form within large organizations. However, they are often encouraged (either knowingly or unknowingly) when the incentive structure rewards individual success. As an example, it is common for companies to divide each functional area into its own profit center. The intent may be to keep the functional leaders and teams more accountable for their own success. However, an unintended outcome can often be silo creation and competition between the internal teams for recognition and resources.

Over the years, we have observed that most business teams and organizations do not need to be taught to be more competitive. Instead, learning how to be more collaborative is a much harder lesson for most teams. The good news is that collaboration has been gaining traction with the more progressive, modern leaders. It starts at the top by creating a culture of sharing best practices and freely communicating across functional areas to eliminate silos.

The hard work of breaking down the silos needs to be supported with the proper incentives. It may be as simple as changing the reward structure from individual profit centers to companywide profit sharing.

It is imperative for the leader of the company to make this change a priority. When a team is operating from the center – a healthy balance of collaboration and competition – they are "in flow" or "in the zone," and winning becomes second nature.

INDOOR LESSON

In my thirty years of management, I have led hundreds of quarterly sales meetings. Early on, I decided to change the routine and rename *meetings* to *workshop and retreat to recharge*. The intention was to refocus the team's energy around getting some "work" done and putting the "charge" back into our step. My belief is that words matter, and in fact, words are what separate us from other primates.

Traditionally, sales meetings focus on reporting up from the field reps to the management team. Sales reps too often try to filter the key facts so as not to expose any potential performance issues. In quarterly updates, the status reports of "average" and "on-track" are often the targeted norm.

The focus of a sales workshop and retreat to recharge is much different. First, the shift is from focusing on the individual sales territory to focusing on the larger district, regional, national, and even international territory. Second, the shift is from a heavy weight of competition (sales reps competing against other reps) toward the middle with much more collaboration among the whole team. Here is the outline of a sales workshop and retreat:

- Review company values, vision, and mission
- Review and recommit to team goals
- Sales territory updates by sales reps
  - Review YTD sales versus plan
  - Share on-track lessons
  - Share off-track lessons
  - Corrective plan
- Share best practices from territory
- Team-building exercise

Obviously, the agenda changes based on the season and specific company initiatives, but we are confident these core elements will elevate your sales team. Other teams – for example, finance or engineering – can readily adopt this workshop agenda to review the status of projects, share best practices, and so forth. In fact, we always include best practices, because this is often a missing component in virtually any type of team (particularly sales teams).

Sharing best practices is essential to increase collaboration and move the competitive weight toward the balance of the middle.

I often hear from competitive sales teams that there is no incentive to help others, and all the incentive is focused on maximizing sales revenue in the individual territory. This certainly has been true in most old-school sales teams that are out of balance. My belief is that more and more sales leaders understand the importance of collaboration in the modern workplace and have added team incentives to encourage collaboration.

I have asked top-performing sales reps this question: "What is the downside to sharing best practices?" The typical response: "If I give my teammates my good ideas, then I will lose my status as top dog."

My response is to keep mining: "Why does giving a best practice to another territory hurt your territory?" The answer: "Well, it might not, but why should I give away a good idea without getting one back in return?" Let's dig into this response, because this is often the mentality that is keeping teams from excellence.

Based on our previous discussion, this is clearly an opportunity to teach the team about abundance versus scarcity. I have found that in many American teams, the concept toward a trade is deeply rooted. A deep-seated belief is that I can only give my teammate a good idea if I receive another good idea in return. Clearly a trade is not pure collaboration. For it to be pure, one needs to believe that by sending out a good idea or doing a good deed, it may someday come back in the gift of another good deed – but there is no guarantee. Pure collaboration relies on faith, trust, and goodwill.

Teaching a team to be more collaborative is hard work. It is also paramount in any team's journey to becoming centered and reaching the top.

OUTDOOR LESSON #1

As stated in earlier chapters, we can often learn more from the poorly performing leaders and teams than the great ones. We will start with a few stories that show teams out of balance.

Early in our business we were hired by a *Fortune* 500 company based in the Bay Area and a world leader in enterprise software. The company was holding an incentive program for top performers in its U.S. sales organization. After talking with the meeting planner, we knew this would be a top-shelf adventure, but I became uncomfortable once I heard the leader's idea of team building.

The adventure request was completely misguided by design. The incentive meeting would be held at a mid-mountain lodge at 8,400 feet in elevation called Canyons Resort in Park City, Utah. Our guides would lead the twenty-five or so business leaders safely to the summit of the tallest nearby peak at just under 10,000 feet above sea level. We had been promised by the HR department that the group was very fit and made up of runners and triathlon athletes. The participants would race to the top with the best man/woman winning. He/she would be rewarded by the CEO in person, as he would fly his helicopter to the peak and await the victor.

This raised a series of big, red flags. Here are just of few:

- Most of the guests would be arriving from sea level, and this event was scheduled for the second day. Ideally, we would allow time for guests to acclimate to the elevation to avoid altitude sickness.
- How could we keep the guests safe on our watch?
- One winner and twenty-four losers is not team building.
- Pressure from the CEO made this adventure far from a "free choice" for the participants.

If this request had come later in my career, I would have clearly said, "No thanks." Unfortunately, we took the job and challenged our internal team to pull it off. We did reply to the meeting planner with four non-negotiables:

1. Guests could opt-out and not participate based on choice (as with all of our adventures).
2. We would create rope teams of four, so it truly would be a team event. (Each team of four would be tethered together for safety reasons and to promote team building.)
3. We would send guests a thirty-day training schedule, so they would understand the challenge and physically could prepare for the race.
4. We asked that the adventure be scheduled for the third day of their visit, so guests could acclimate to the high altitude.

After our initial welcome email to participants, we told them the event was by choice and their responses would be confidential. Several guests immediately opted out of the competition due to various ailments. We ended up with sixteen guests randomly selected into four teams of four racers.

Our guide team performed at a high level, and we got all four teams to the summit without any significant injuries or issues. The company performance was not a surprise as they were likely the most competitive team we had ever worked with. However, the leadership style and company culture were a surprise.

When the first team arrived exhausted at the peak, they were quite surprised to see a helicopter and even more surprised to see their CEO. After a few high fives, he said: "Welcome to the top. What took you so long?" They had a few disingenuous laughs as they waited for the other teams to arrive.

We all gathered for the climatic CEO speech. It was short and not-so-sweet: "We began the year with a simple message: Conquer the summit. Now we have done that as both individuals and as a company. However, there can only be one winner. Congrats to team three!" He then passed out four envelopes to the winning team members. Inside were American Express travel certificates for an all-paid vacation for two. He then said his goodbyes and made the quick and loud exit that only an inflated ego can.

I had a chance to speak with the VP of sales on the way down the mountain to the lodge. She thanked me for making the event such a success. She added that she wanted to share some learnings with the team that came out of the rope team concept of being tethered together.

I asked her about the CEO's antics with the helicopter. She replied: "That is just John being John. We love him."

I asked boldly, "I bet you do, but do you respect his leadership style?"

She paused and then said, "We hope the company never loses his ultra-competitive spirit that has made us so successful, but we are slowly trying to become a more balanced company." I asked how. "The board of directors has intentionally been bringing in more diverse and seasoned professional managers to help us become more mature and well rounded."

I was pleased to hear that and encouraged her to pass along the message that they should keep learning and growing. I joined the VP in leading a solid debrief back at the lodge and trusted that some of the lessons from the mountain would help them fuse into a better, more collaborative team back at work.

In contrast, let's look at a story from the other end of the spectrum – a team that is too heavily weighted toward collaboration with virtually no competitive edge.

OUTDOOR LESSON #2

Sundance is one of my favorite alpine destinations in the world. It's a small village at the base of Mount Timpanogos and truly a slice of heaven. A beauty and wellness company hired Park City Teamworks to run an outdoor adventure that would connect its management team to nature. We chose our Alpine Discovery adventure and designed a course at the Nordic center, which makes for a moderate adventure with spectacular scenery in the summer.

As we began the brief session, a quick scan of our guests revealed that we had a diverse group of both gender and race. This was a refreshing change from our normal, "pale and male" team makeup. After a few inquiries, we discovered our guests were mostly former salon managers who had been promoted to positions at the corporate office. Of note, they were also standing out as a vocal and ruckus crowd.

We designed Alpine Discovery with two primary and competing goals:

1. Be the individual team with the most points.
2. Be the company to beat the corporate average for total combined points by all teams.

A team has to accomplish both goals in order to win. We believe this mirrors the balance of competition and collaboration required at the workplace.

On a spectacular August day in the mountains, the bell sounded, and the teams were off on their adventure. For most corporate groups this means a running start with a high level of competitive juice. Not this group.

One of the leaders secured the entire group's attention and asked, "What are we trying to accomplish today? Beat the corporate average? Does that really matter? How about we simply work together to have fun, build relationships, and connect with nature?" The instant reply was a loud cheer of approval.

My initial thought was, *This is going to be interesting.* But as consultants we always encourage our clients to play the way they normally play and try not to influence their behavior with our biases. Off the group went laughing and walking down the trail enjoying themselves.

Two and a half hours later all the teams returned to Base Camp with the same high energy and good spirits. They held true to their strategy of sharing and having fun. Throughout the adventure, they shared experiences and busted on each other in a well-natured way. It was truly hard to argue with their collaborative nature.

During our debrief, they shared a bunch of learnings that would make them better as both individuals and teams. Then the moment of truth – we shared the results. They were one of the lowest performing companies of all time in regard to point total. Surprisingly, this was met with a loud cheer from the crowd.

I responded with probing questions to test their resolve: "Would you have changed anything if we had given you the team point total for Este Lauder, a huge competitor?" A chorus of "Boo!" rang out.

The leader walked up, asked for the microphone, and said, "You bet that would have made all the difference. Does anyone here think we wouldn't have crushed the EL team score?" Sure enough, a loud roar thundered from the crowd of proud employees.

My parting words were simple: "You guys were one of the most collaborative teams we have ever worked with. It is also clear that you have a special company culture. Cherish and protect those things. I know you are very successful, and I sense that you also have a special competitive spirit. We did not really witness that today on the mountain, so we will leave you with the challenge to make sure you play in the middle with a good balance of competing externally and collaborating internally."

Now that we have looked at a couple of teams out of balance, let's look at a team that distinguished itself as a centered team with a healthy balance of collaboration and competition.

OUTDOOR LESSON #3

Deer Valley has a storied history of being the number-one ski resort in North America by providing unparalleled guest services. This region has some of the best hotels and corporate meeting facilities around, so it attracts a fair number of high-end guests and companies.

A top biotech and pharmaceutical company from southern California and the United Kingdom hired Park City Teamworks to provide a business adventure for its global high-potential leaders. Over the years, we have worked with many biotech firms and have come to admire their highly competitive spirit. In our experience, these sales and marketing teams are made up of type-A folks who tip toward the competitive end of the scale.

We could sense a different nature from this group as soon as we met them outside their lodge on a beautiful fall afternoon with the aspen trees in their full golden glory. Their leaders chose one of my favorite adventures: Circle of Life, a teepee building experience.

We design the event with a hidden lesson. We break the group into three small teams and secretly provide each team with different instructions to build three twenty-foot shelters. Collectively, the three teams have all the information they need to properly build the structures, if they choose to collaborate. Individually, each team has limited instructions – a handicap if the three teams focus on competing with each other.

Here is a brief explanation of this outdoor adventure:

1. *A team of visionary leaders* – This team simply receives a photograph of a completed teepee with the line "Go for it."
2. *A team of best-practice leaders* – This team receives a professionally condensed version of the most important nine steps with diagrams.
3. *A team of bureaucratic leaders* – This team receives a fifty-three-page book of instructions with way too much information.

By now you should see how this event can reveal learnings, which participants can take back to their company. If the leaders don't share information, then you will see three very different outcomes from the teams.

This company did not fall for the normal trap of having too much competitive spirit. We explained the dual goals of:

1. Be the team that builds their teepee first.
2. As a company, beat the corporate average from all the companies who have previously participated in this event.

The bell rang for the start of the timed event. This is historically met with a mad rush to the various bags of equipment and a bunch of chaos. It was different this time. The group of twenty-five participants – everyone in all three teams – calmly met in the middle and metaphorically took a step back to see the challenge from a wider view. They asked if anyone had ever built a teepee before – a great question. The answer was no, but they quickly self-selected three team leaders to organize a plan of attack.

Next, they asked us an important question: "What is the best time you have ever seen?" We answered fourteen minutes. Ok, they now had a clear target, and they also knew what was possible.

Next, they calmly gathered all the information and made an action plan for the three teams to build the three teepees. They took out their cell phones and took three sets of photos of the key instructions – the most useful document with brief instructions and diagrams.

The three leaders ran back and forth between the three sites, shared helpful information, and assisted as needed to ensure none of the teams fell behind. It was a truly amazing experience to watch excellence in action.

Boom! All three teepees were standing at thirteen minutes and fifteen seconds. A new record for Park City Teamworks! They handily beat the corporate average of twenty-two minutes and the previous record of fourteen minutes. A confident celebration by the entire group ensued as we gathered in one of the shelters for the debrief.

My first question: "Which team got their teepee up first?"

Everyone looked around, and someone said, "We don't really know, but we can tell you that we broke the world record as a collective group."

Hard to argue the facts, however, it's my job as a performance consultant to keep pushing back. "How could you have done better?"

The group brainstormed a few ideas for efficiency improvements that mostly centered around better communication. Everyone agreed that the leadership and strategy were straight on.

There is a bunch of learning to unpack from that amazing fall day in the Wasatch Mountains. The greatest of which is the power of a team that has a spirit balanced in the middle of the competitive and collaborative spectrum.

HOMEWORK/TEAM TALK

One thing we have found to be true over the years is that we rarely had to teach American teams to be more competitive, because they play well above the midline. The following discussions will help your team become more centered.

1. Identify where your team sits on the collaboration-competition spectrum with a subjective self-assessment. Have each team member independently record a number between one and ten where one is extremely collaborative, five is the middle point, and ten is extremely competitive. (Keep in mind that you want your team to compete outside your organization and collaborate inside your organization.)

2. Share the results and calculate the average score for the team. Then go around the circle and share some examples of why the score makes sense or doesn't make sense.

3. If you're not satisfied with the results and want to find ways to grow and move closer to the center, then use a white board to brainstorm tangible ways to improve. The list should include ways to find more win-win solutions that promote internal collaboration.

4. Lastly, assign a situational leader to drive better and more collaborative results. Keep in mind that your Relating-themed team members will have the best strengths aligned with collaboration. And, as noted earlier, women tend to be better collaborators than men. Trust that they will be the best to lead this exercise.

We wish you all the best in your quest to be a more centered team with elevated performance.

Circle of Life, native american teepee building at Sundance Mountain Resort

CHAPTER 5

COMMUNITY SUMMIT – Nurture Trust, Caring, and Sharing

OVER THE YEARS, OUR PARK CITY TEAMWORKS TEAM has gone back and forth on naming this summit either *community* or *communication*. We have witnessed that winning teams have an authentic sense of caring for each other, much like a family. And in practice they care enough about each other that they display an authentic openness in the way they share and communicate. Simply put, they trust each other enough to have difficult conversations. We settled on *community,* because it is broader and encompasses communication.

One of the first things you notice about the two words is that they share the first seven letters: *communi.* I knew my college Latin class would someday come in handy. Let's look at the Latin roots of these two words: From the Latin, the noun *communis* means "common, public, shared by all or many." Similarly, the verb *communicare* means "make something common."

This is likely why we struggled with the two titles. Let's start with the idea of *community.* Community at work has a wide spectrum of perspectives from a small, five-person functional team to the massive online communities with thousands, if not millions, of members. Common to all of these communities is a group of motivated individuals, organized around a common cause larger than themselves. It is human nature to seek connections and a sense of belonging in larger tribes.

THE 7 SUMMITS OF WINNING TEAMS
Winning teams are, have, or use:

CHIEF	=	Served by a 4S Leader
CHEMISTRY	=	Diversity of Thought and Complementary Skills
COMPASS	=	Common Purpose, Alignment, and Destination
CENTERED	=	Balance of Competition and Collaboration
COMMUNITY	**=**	**Trust, Care, and Share**
CREATIVITY	=	Solutions from Within
COURAGE	=	Overcome Adversity and Challenge the Status Quo

Why might you care and invest resources in building a sense of community for your team? When team members feel a sense of belonging:

- They have a greater sense of dedication.
- They take less time off work.
- They are more likely to demonstrate loyalty, display high levels of creativity and productivity, and inspire others to adopt the same attitude.
- In a competitive talent market, this is a successful strategy to attract and retain key talent.

Our primary focus will be on the smaller work teams. For the more than 2,500 business teams we have worked with, most of the high-performing teams demonstrated a strong sense of family that has been shaped by both time and challenge. Much like a steel sword, their sense of community has been tempered by fire and sharpened on stone.

Think back to all the great teams you have been part of, and I bet you will recall the team fighting through some early adversity – a rough patch, a large challenge, something that forced the team to dig deep and find a way out. I believe that when your team is in this "purgatory" you either fall into failure or rise above to success.

When we interview these winning teams and ask them what "secret sauce" gives them such a strong sense of community, we hear common themes:

- We *trust* each other.
- We *care* about each other like extended family.
- We openly *share* good and bad news.

Let's look at a comprehensive study performed by Google in 2012, named Project Aristotle. In a quest to build better teams within Google, the executives assembled a team of researchers to sift through decades of data on teams and study more than 100 teams within their workforce of 50,000 employees.

For a company renowned for its ability to process data, the researchers found it hard to quantify what made the best teams work. The researchers did find two team norms that were common in all the best teams:

- First, members expressed themselves in meetings in roughly the same proportion. For example, introverts didn't remain silent while extroverts ruled the meeting. Researchers referred to this phenomenon as "equality in distribution of conversational turn-taking."
- Second, the good teams all had higher than average "social sensitivity" – a fancy way of saying they were skilled at intuiting how others felt based on their tone of voice and their expressions and other nonverbal cues.

Those of us in the team-building and high-performance field find it paradoxical that Google's intense data collection in Project Aristotle led it to a fairly obvious conclusion: In the best teams, members listen to one another, care about each other, and are sensitive to each other's feelings and needs.

This research confirms our belief that winning teams must possess the soft skills above the hard skills. At the core, this requires each team member to sacrifice the ME for the WE.

Now that we have talked about community and winning teams, let's pivot to looking at what winning teams do: They share and communicate at a high level.

Our research from working with 40,000 business leaders over twenty years shows that the best-performing teams are those that communicate the best. Winning teams have the ability to communicate freely and openly. They do not hold back and internalize what they are truly feeling. In my experience, it is not what gets *said* that hurts teams – instead it is what gets left *unsaid* that is most harmful.

When team members have the courage and permission to say what is on their minds, then the team's shared knowledge grows with time. When we ask teams what drives open communication, the responses center around *leadership*, *culture*, and *time*:

- The *leader* builds a safe environment for open communication and then practices open communication over time.
- This builds trust within the team and leads to a *culture* of openness.
- Finally, there is no replacement for experience and *time*. Teams only get better at communication with practice and time. Perfect.

Highly communicative teams do not just share good news and positive feedback. In fact, the best teams share the hard news and give constructive feedback equally well. This follows the "what is unsaid" statement mentioned earlier. When a teammate holds back from giving feedback, then they own it by keeping it internal. It stays inside and typically grows in magnitude over time. It is human nature to believe that being kind and nice helps to build relationships. This is true. However, relationships can only grow when the hard issues are tackled too.

CARABINER KEY POINT:

I have learned these two lessons through hard experiences: 1) Difficult conversations only become harder if left to fester over time, and 2) difficult conversations always feel better behind you rather than in front of you.

One of my favorite books that addresses team communication is *Crucial Conversations: Learn Effective Communication Skills* by my fellow Utahans at VitalSmarts. (I have had the privilege to work with one of the authors, Ron McMillan, and a few of his adult children have helped to facilitate and guide our business adventures. They are a special family.)

According to this book, a crucial conversation has three elements: high stakes, varying opinions, and strong emotions. Using this definition, hardly a week goes by in our workplace or home life that doesn't include a crucial conversation.

Yet why do most adult professionals avoid difficult conversations? It is part of human nature to avoid these challenges through "flight" with the hope that problems will simply go away. They rarely do. The good news is that better, more effective communication is a learned behavior that can be taught and practiced.

In fact, *Crucial Conversations* points out that effective communication is the only reliable path to resolve issues instead of avoiding them or handling them poorly. That seems simple enough. Walk away from crucial conversations and suffer the consequences. Handle them poorly and suffer the consequences. Or handle them well with effective communication, resolve the situation, and improve the relationship.

We all know the quality of our life at home, work, and in the community relies on the quality of our relationships. The answer to our options in how to handle difficult conversations is number three – face them and handle them well.

Over decades of research with thousands of companies, the authors of *Crucial Conversations* have given us a clear path to learn how to handle these situations well. We strongly encourage you to read their book, and if you are leading a team then hire VitalSmarts to teach one of their workshops.

Here is just one of the many lessons I have taken away from the book and practices over the years to help me and the teams I work with perform at a higher level. The first step to achieve the best results in a crucial conversation at work is to arrive at the engagement with an openness to learn and an authentic belief that the best result has a positive win-win outcome for both parties. If you try to achieve a more competitive win-lose outcome, then I suggest you reserve your competitive conversations for those outside the organization. Remember, collaborate inside your group, and compete outside your organization.

The authors of *Crucial Conversations* teach us that the most skilled communicators are 100 percent honest while being 100 percent respectful as they work toward true dialogue.

My guess is that the authors were very intentional in choosing 100 percent for both honesty and respect. There is not much wiggle room when things get crucial. Also, the term *dialogue* is critical to better outcomes. Of course, a larger shared pool of information will lead to better decisions, which is critical to becoming a high-performing team. Yet our experience at the workplace is often the opposite. All too often, we seek to be right and dig in on our own ideas and try to convince others rather than seeking true dialogue.

Effective communication is challenging and requires awareness and practice. At Park City Teamworks we humorously say, "Communication is simple – until human beings get in the way."

In conclusion, we hope you have learned about the power of community in building and being part of a winning team. It's hard work and takes time, but there is no better feeling than to be part of a team that openly communicates and treats each other with total honesty and mutual respect. We will finish this summit with examples from in the office and on the mountain.

INDOOR LESSON

I have been blessed to have worked for companies that have a strong sense of community, and I would like to think that as a leader I helped to contribute to their unique cultures. Many years ago, I was asked to consider an executive position for a water-management company in New England. At the time, my young family was living and thriving in the mountains of Utah. I was the western sales manager and co-led all the sales efforts with a colleague based in Florida. Together, we had built a sales force of thirty-five to forty professionals who shared a passion for hard work and having fun while doing it. We helped to drive sales growth of more than 500 percent in a five-year period.

The privately held company was founded by a brilliant inventor who had built the company on a culture of innovation. In that year, we were launching a new product line in the stormwater market. It truly was a game changer and was poised to revolutionize a second industry for the young company.

Prior to the product launch, our sales team pre-sold millions of dollars in designs across the country. This was a massive success for such a small company and for a product that had yet to be produced.

We launched the new product that spring, and by summer we had field crews traveling across the country installing our stormwater systems on new commercial job sites. By August, we had more than twenty installations and a two-year backlog of orders in our sales pipeline. What could possibly go wrong?

In fact, just about everything went wrong. Within a matter of weeks nearly all of our systems were in some degree of trouble, and many had reached total failure. Many of these job sites were projects with some of the largest retailers in the nation.

These early management meetings were definitely the most intense meetings of my career. There was a ton of emotions with everything from finger-pointing to covering your backside. This problem had all the makings of a crucial conversation.

Once the initial smoke cleared, cooler heads prevailed, and we realized we were clearly out of our league and needed professional advice. We interviewed and retained some of the best law firms and public relation firms in New York City specializing in bankruptcy law.

Our team got a crash course in bankruptcy law, and it was clear that the only path forward was Chapter 11 bankruptcy protection. We were a profitable company, but we now had liabilities from lawsuits that largely outweighed our assets. We were assured by our consultants that they would steer us through the difficult few years, and we would have a solid chance to come out of bankruptcy with a healthy company going forward.

I don't need to go into details on the bankruptcy case for obvious reasons, but this situation did have a successful ending for the company and its creditors. The better part of the story and certainly the more relevant part was how we led our teams through the change. This challenge would rock us to our core and test our strong sense of community.

During one of our first leadership meetings, we were asked by our PR consultants who would lead the messaging to our sales force and, eventually, to our customers. Because we had split the country into two zones, this was a difficult decision. Ultimately, our president chose me – a young sales manager who had helped build our strong sense of community. I was honored to accept such a tall mountain to climb.

My most difficult sales job would be convincing my wife to move our family, so I could metaphorically captain the *Titanic* after it had already hit the iceberg. God bless her, she also knew I was the right leader for the job.

Our PR professionals helped us develop a solid plan with priorities. We agreed that our first priority for the sales team was to make sure none of our key team members or distribution partners jumped ship. Even before we went out to our customers with a positive spin, we needed our sales team to make the difficult decision to commit to staying with the company and seeing this through.

We held an all-hands-on-deck meeting for the entire sales team. The first day was designed to be educational. We needed to educate our team on the details of our Chapter 11 filing and make the distinction between restructuring and the more ominous Chapter 7 filing that is a more common public reference.

As you can imagine, this went long into the night, as most of the forty or so sales folks really just wanted to know "What's in it for me?" They rightfully were tuned into "radio station WIIFM."

That morning before breakfast, a few of my senior people grouped the sales reps into three lists: low risk, medium risk, and high risk. Ten sales reps made the third list – folks who, most likely, would not want to stay on board and see this thing through until we could right the ship. I knew my personal, number-one priority as the leader was to visit each of these sales reps with their families as soon as possible. These were going to be crucial conversations – big time.

For the next week, we flew around the country meeting with families in person to listen to them and answer their questions. Our eastern zone manager handled the meetings on the East Coast, because he had earned the trust of his team members.

The meetings were very long and difficult with high emotions, but I am proud to say we only lost two sales reps out of nearly forty on our team. While it appeared that we accomplished this during the week from hell, it was actually due to the investment we had made in our people in the previous five years of building a strong sense of community in our sales team.

The story has a happy ending. The company emerged from Chapter 11 in just a few short years, and the owners were proud to pay back our creditors in whole. Once the ship was stable, I made the difficult decision to leave that team to start my own company. I remain fortunate to have had those critical business experiences – and crucial conversations – at such a young age. I am still proud of the team we built and the work we accomplished. Two decades later, many of my friends are still with that business, and they remain an integral part of a successful, industry-leading company.

OUTDOOR LESSON

My favorite team-building story where community was on display happened one winter at Snowbasin Ski Resort in Utah. We were hired to provide an outdoor activity with a leadership team of fifteen folks from the state health department. We selected our Mountain Survival adventure and suggested we use snowshoes given the 200 inches of snow the Wasatch Mountains had received that season.

We selected a beautiful alpine canyon at the base of Snowbasin that is used for cross-country skiing and snowshoeing. During our interview, the leader selected a low-to-mid level of fitness for her team, and we knew this course would be a good match and still be a home run for scenery.

Three days prior to the event, we sent our preparatory team email and reported that the weather report was for snow, so please plan to dress appropriately. We received a larger than normal number of concerned emails from the participants. This lowered the bar for my expectations for this team and the event.

On the way to the event, my eldest son and I were getting excited, because Mother Nature was blessing us with a dump of the "best snow on earth." We arrived early and set three GPS locations down the canyon for our favorite winter team-building challenges in this Mountain Survival adventure. The three challenges were:

1. Conduct a search-and-rescue scenario.
2. Build a shelter/snow cave.
3. Conduct a mock avalanche rescue.

We returned to Base Camp and waited for everyone to arrive. As usual, holding the briefing during a snowstorm or any harsh weather condition is met with a higher degree of anxiety. Over the years, as guides, we learned to welcome adversity, because we knew it led to the best adventures and lessons. After fitting everyone with snowshoes and ski poles, our two teams slid and stumbled down the snowy path.

We like snowshoe events, because they tend to be the "great equalizer" – everyone is a bit uncomfortable on snowshoes, even the cocky weekend athletes. The other noteworthy thing about this group is that they seemed to all be great friends and knew each other well enough to spend most of the prep time busting on each other with good humor and well-intentioned jest.

During our first two challenges, I was impressed with my team's performance. They shared leadership based on experience and pushed each other for results. Our communication leader was also communicating with the other team and sharing some best practices and even "worst practices" regarding what not to do. The event was exceeding my expectations until, suddenly, I received a radio call from my son, who was guiding one of the teams.

Someone on his team had suffered an injury at the third challenge – avalanche rescue. He was calm, and being a trained ski patroller/first responder, he had everything under control. He relayed the patient's name and reassured everyone that she was going to be fine. She had slipped down a small embankment while performing the probe line, somehow got her snowshoe twisted under her body, and badly sprained her left ankle.

My team overheard the bad news over the radio and immediately said, "Team member down; we are on our way." We quickly cleaned up our challenge and double-timed it to the avalanche station. I had been super-impressed with the team dynamic and now even more so under stress. They remained calm and continued to ask excellent questions as we stomped down the snowy path. We all knew the key element of the rescue was going to be the evacuation, as the avalanche station was the farthest from Base Camp and our vehicles.

Upon our arrival, my son's team had already been performing at a high level. The victim was in a makeshift rescue stretcher, packed with extra jackets for warmth, and had a solid SAM Splint on her ankle. Again, super impressed that teammates had taken off their jackets during a snowstorm to lend them to the person in need. We probably should not have been surprised that a team from the state health department had tons of medical experience.

If there is a medical event on the mountain during a Park City Teamworks adventure, we make the patient's safety a priority, but we also have to make sure our other guests get back to Base Camp safely as well. We accomplish this by "dividing and conquering" our team with the two main priorities. Because of the smaller group size and the committed nature of this group, I decided to lead the solutions dialogue with the entire group. I knew they could handle this conversation, and their medical and leadership experience would add to arriving at the best solution.

I listed the facts as I saw them:

1. Our injury assessment was an ankle sprain, not a break.
2. We were more than two miles from Base Camp and the vehicles.
3. It was snowing, we only had eighty minutes of daylight left, and the temperature was dropping.

4. My professional guess was that we were a sixty-minute snowshoe to Base Camp, given we would be pulling a sled with our patient.
5. We would not have cell service until we got closer to Base Camp.

Our options were:

1. We could stay put while my son would triple-time it back to near Base Camp where we last had cell service and call ski patrol to request a snowmobile evacuation.
2. We could all stick together and take turns pulling our patient's sled back to Base Camp. And before I could even consider a third option, most of the team said, "We aren't getting any closer by standing here, and we are not leaving any team member behind – ever." Our injured guest concurred.

This was top-shelf team building under the worst conditions. We did have one addition to our plan. My son would run ahead and warm the Land Rover to prepare for an evacuation at the trailhead. He would also call ski patrol to inform them of the incident and tell them we planned to use our vehicle to take our patient to the nearest first-aid station.

As we trekked down the path to safety, the patient started singing Christmas carols and everyone joined in to pass the time. We continually switched out the sled pullers based on people's size and strength. A team I had prematurely lowered the bar on was quickly becoming one of my favorite groups of all time.

We arrived at the vehicle in excellent time and in excellent spirits. The patient insisted that we should not call ski patrol for assistance, and upon further inspection with better light in the truck, we saw that her ankle did not have signs of significant swelling. No super-tender spots and even some limited movement. In our opinion, she was going to be fine – it was most likely a sprain, not a break – but our company protocol required a trip to the hospital.

She thanked everyone and then asked if our protocol required her to go to the hospital immediately or if could she wait until after the debrief in the warm lodge with her team. We reluctantly agreed with the patient's wishes and drove to the lodge for a warm fire, hot cocoa, and a lively debrief discussion. The team quickly figured out carpool logistics and who would go with her to the hospital after the debrief – the whole works, including a team call to the husband asking what he wanted for Christmas other than serving his wife while she recovered.

The day ended on a positive note with a negative X-ray at the hospital. More importantly, seventeen adults learned about the power of community and teamwork. Together we can always accomplish more than we can alone.

Mountain Survival, team celebration in Wasatch Mountains

HOMEWORK/TEAM TALK

Building a team with a strong sense of community with people who care enough about each other to share open and honest communication takes time. This means creating a variety of support systems and events that encourage employees to get to know each other and collaborate effectively.

Some employees may gain a sense of cohesion from social activities while others are more responsive to working as a unit to achieve a common objective. Offering a variety of activities allows team members to select the ones that work best for them.

I have found that the best way to expedite the time for a team to gain a sense of community is for the team members to spend more time together away from the workplace. I like to call it *real time*. I have also found that taking the team through team-building adventures and service experiences are excellent ways to shorten the time it takes to build a sense of community. As we have learned, adversity in completing challenging outdoor events is a great teacher. Plus, here are a few ideas you can explore to build community:

1. Trade in the traditional golf outings for outdoor team-building adventures. Most cities and corporate meeting locations are served by adventure companies that can be hired for their adventure permits, experience, and safety.

2. A few of my favorite adventures for business teams include:
   a. River rafting
   b. Orienteering
   c. Canyoneering
   d. Rock climbing/rappelling
   e. Night hikes with headlamps
   f. Survival challenges

3. Service work through local nonprofit organizations is also an excellent way to build teams and help your local community by connecting everyone through a shared sense of achievement. Take a break in your busy day to stop and look around for groups in your community that need your team's help. Here are a few ideas for excellent team-building activities:
   a. Help to build a house with Habitat for Humanity.

    b.   Assemble bikes or jungle gyms for local children's shelters.

    c.   Cook and serve meals for a homeless shelter and others in need by working with your local churches, synagogues, and mosques.

4.   Create group networks. When people have something in common, they are more likely to connect. Here are a few ideas:

    a.   Start a company softball, volleyball, or kickball team at your local recreation league.

    b.   Put a team together to participate in a local charity fun run or walkathon.

    c.   And one of my all-time favorites – challenge ten to twelve workmates to sign up for a 200-mile Ragnar Relay, a life-changing experience. Learn more at www.RunRagnar.com.

5.   Recognition through awards programs can help to stimulate a sense of community in your team. Recognition can create a strong sense of purpose and belonging as well as give employees a good excuse to come together and celebrate.

Lastly, we believe one of the true tests for a high level of community within your team is a positive answer to this question: *Can you truly call your teammates at work your friends?* We wish you all the best in your team's journey to the top.

CREATIVITY SUMMIT – Discover Solutions from Within

THE SIXTH COMMON TRAIT we have witnessed in winning teams is that they are highly creative and have the collective power from within to solve problems and overcome obstacles. Creativity is the precursor to innovation. *Creativity* is the thought while *innovation* is an outcome of that thought.

THE 7 SUMMITS OF WINNING TEAMS

Winning teams are, have, or use:

CHIEF	=	Served by a 4S Leader
CHEMISTRY	=	Diversity of Thought and Complementary Skills
COMPASS	=	Common Purpose, Alignment, and Destination
CENTERED	=	Balance of Competition and Collaboration
COMMUNITY	=	Trust, Care, and Share
CREATIVITY	=	**Solutions from Within**
COURAGE	=	Overcome Adversity and Challenge the Status Quo

Even though the two terms are often linked together, they actually utilize two different parts of the brain. It's long been thought that the right side of the brain is used for creative thought, and the left side is used for more linear thinking including processing the idea. The common belief that the right side of the brain is primarily responsible for creativity may actually be a myth.

Modern neuroscience has begun to map the brain and study its functions using magnetic resonance imagery (MRI). Researchers have confirmed that the human brain has as many as 86 billion neurons, and each neuron makes many synapses or connections during specific tasks or actions.

This brain mapping has confirmed that highly creative activity is coming from as many as forty areas of the brain and from both the right and left hemispheres – confirming that the right-side-only creative brain is, in fact, a myth.

The Cognitive Neuroscience Creativity Lab at Penn State has been studying the creative brain by asking the million-dollar question: Can creativity be enhanced?

The lab's research is still early, and our ability to enhance our creativity in the long-term will need further research. However, some of the studies are revealing short-term benefits. Until the science on creativity uncovers specific answers to the question, the research team suggests taking a break if you're stuck on a problem, which actually "loosens things up" and helps you find a creative solution to your problem. In addition, they suggest picking up a creative hobby – music, art, and so forth – to boost your creativity.

We are just scratching the surface of what we can learn from brain-mapping research. For now, one thing is clear: There are no shortcuts or magic pills that can make your team more creative. It requires hard work and an open mind.

Building a more creative team starts with a good leader. The leader must lay out the proper canvas for the collective genius of the team to thrive and create. In his more than twenty-five years studying creativity in the healthcare industry, Michael West outlines the five common traits of creative teams in his TED Talk:

- **Vision** – They are driven by a common desire to grow.
- **The dance** – They practice the art of reflection.
- **Team diversity** – They have a diversity of thought.
- **Positivity** – They have a belief of optimism and hope.
- **Quality** – They push each other to be great.

Many of these traits can be found in some of the previous summits we discussed, but my two favorites are *the dance* and *positivity*. West defines *the dance* as a common practice that winning teams use to become more creative – they practice the art of reflection. They take time to stop and look back on an event or project and simply ask themselves what they can learn to get better. This type of reflective learning is purely human and separates us from the rest of the animal kingdom. Reflection requires a belief and passion in constant, never-ending improvement.

For the past twenty years, Park City Teamworks has ended each of our outdoor adventures with a debrief session. To help guide these sessions, we created the acronym ART:

A = Adventure, a journey to the unknown

R = Reflection, zoom out and look back at lessons learned

T = Transfer, take the outdoor lessons back to the workplace

Our ART model has proven to be very helpful for work teams to explore the boundaries of creativity. The debrief sessions are held immediately after the adventure when the team members' energy levels are peaked.

It is also our belief that humans can find creative energy by connecting with the outdoors. Mother Nature is a great teacher, so try tapping into her power. If you are struggling with a solution, take a nature hike or hold your next creative session outside on the company's campus.

The simple practice of taking time to regularly reflect back on your team's performance will pay massive dividends. Learning from mistakes and challenging your team to improve on your successes will build a culture of creativity and excellence.

As consultants, we have also found that positivity is a common trait of most high-performing teams. When teams have a positive attitude and approach problems with positive energy, they are gifted with more creative ideas. Hope and positivity trump fear and negativity every time. Teams need to believe they have the solutions within before they actually see the results reveal themselves. In other words, positivity directly impacts creativity.

Before founding Park City Teamworks, I worked for mid-size manufacturing companies selling products and services to end users. Each company would certainly be self-labeled as creative – even innovative – and they were industry leaders. From a global perspective, it would be a stretch to call them innovative across all industries. A fair assessment would be that they were clearly growth oriented.

It is my firm belief that there is no stasis in business. Teams and companies are either dying or growing. If there is a middle ground, then it is short lived and simply means you are transitioning from one state to the other.

Growing companies and teams have the primary aim of either entering new markets or gaining new market share. It is the growth mindset that drives the need for creativity and innovation.

Even though most business leaders know that creativity and innovation are critical to successful growth, it is shocking that so many companies are so poor at being creative. My belief is that we can blame our traditional education system for this. We start kindergarten with a ton of creative potential and the creative freedom to explore with building blocks, art projects, and outdoor play. However, it doesn't take our structured educational system long to place our children in the confines of a desk with structured lesson plans.

Corporate America tends to follow this structured process in the work environment. In our outdoor adventures, we often see teams that are creatively blocked. To move through the blocks, we ask team members to reflect on whether their company's processes and leadership are truly inspiring them to tap into their best ideas and limitless creative potential.

Often, business processes and the work environment are too structured to unleash the free flow of truly disruptive ideas. When team members feel they lack the flexibility or safety to express ideas that are counter to standard processes – or the way things have traditionally been done – they often revert to conservative thinking that offers only incremental change.

We can all learn how *not* to be more creative from the countless examples of botched brainstorming sessions. Raise your hand if you have seen how *not* to lead a brainstorming session.

Here's how it often plays out: The team leader stands up front with a blank flipchart while everyone sits in their chairs trying to digest a heavy lunch. The team leader starts with a problem statement, writes it at the top of the flipchart, and commands the group to "brainstorm" ideas on how to solve it.

The bold team members begin to shout out a few ideas as the leader asks for more time to write down the ideas. Usually, after just a few ideas, the boss and teammates make the chronic mistakes that stifle creative thinking. They might say:

- "That's a bad/stupid idea."
- "Yeah, but ..."
- "We can't do that."
- "We tried that five years ago, and it didn't work."
- "No way; that will cost too much."

You get the picture and know the poor ending well. The team members' ideas stop flowing, because the environment is no longer free of judgment or a safe place to explore creative ideas. The session quickly turns to groupthink, where the only ideas come from the leader and everyone else simply agrees.

CARABINER KEY POINT:

To facilitate robust experimentation and vigorous healthy debate of ideas, we recommend leaders create an environment of psychological safety.

According to Patricia Riddell, professor of applied neuroscience at the University of Reading, a key to being creative is knowing someone will listen to you without judging you or laughing at you. This is called *psychological safety*. She notes that the real joy of creativity is tossing out a completely outlandish idea, only to realize that "Hey, this might actually work!"

The accountability for building a safe place to explore creative ideas and encouraging healthy conflict and debate lies with the team leader, but once the environment has been set, it is the team's responsibility to continually encourage each other to push their creative limits. Winning teams push beyond their comfort zones to find new ideas and solutions. Remember, creativity leads to innovation.

If your team is struggling to be more creative, then start with the practice of reflection. Keep asking yourselves, "How can we get better?" It is also critical to keep trying new techniques to open up your team members' creative brains. We will share some ideas and tools in our Homework section, which will help to place you on a more creative path.

We are confident that your solutions lie within your team, because no one knows your business better than you do. Be confident in this truth, and then be bold and push the envelope to be more creative and innovative.

INDOOR LESSON

As mentioned previously, one of my last corporate posts was with a mid-size water-management company. For a few years, our executive leadership team struggled to dial-in a compelling vision statement that our employees could attach to and see a larger shared purpose. In fact, we fell for the common trap of changing the vision every year for three straight years. Our intention was good, but the result was poor and simply led to more confusion among our employees.

We accepted the feedback from our employee survey and decided to hire a professional facilitator to help us dial-in a compelling vision statement that we could confidently stand behind for five years or so.

The facilitator began the session by giving some of the more famous examples of vision and purpose statements that successfully paint a clear picture of "Where are we going?"

One of my favorites is the story of President John F. Kennedy asking a NASA employee who was sweeping the floor during a walk-through this question: "Good morning. What is it that you do?"

The response: "I am helping to put a man on the moon before the end of the decade." A perfect reflection of the powerful vision outlined in the President's speech.

The facilitator then introduced our team to a concept called *brain writing* as an elevated replacement for the traditional brainstorming session. Brain writing is designed to eliminate the traps of judgment and groupthink. This process replaces the flipchart or whiteboard at the front of the room with a collection of papers, each with about twenty graphics of empty light bulbs.

Why light bulbs? Because they are the universal symbol of "a great idea," "eureka," and "ah-ha!" The facilitator then gave these instructions: List all the words that come to mind when you think of where your company will be in five years. Simply write any word inside one of the light bulbs. Fill in as many light bulbs as you can in the allotted time and then place your paper in the center of the table. We will complete a series of five rotations. During each rotation, grab a clean sheet of paper, read the ideas from everyone else's papers, and then fill in as many light bulbs as you can during the allotted time." Unlike traditional brainstorming sessions, this exercise is silent.

The concept is simple and powerful. It opens up our brains to creative thinking and allows each team member to build on the ideas of others. At the end of the half-hour session, we had more than 250 words written inside the light bulbs. The facilitator then gathered the papers and, during lunch, had them transcribed into a running list with numbers indicating how many times each word had been written down.

After lunch, the facilitator presented us with the numbered list of approximately 250 words from the brain writing exercise. The next assignment was to individually "rate" our favorite words by placing A, B, or C next to our favorite words (A = excellent, B = very good, C = good). Every person got five votes for each A, B, and C, or fifteen total votes.

At the break, the facilitator collected all of the ratings and then ranked the most popular words. We had about thirty-five highly ranked words with about twenty words that were the clear favorites.

The facilitator then asked us to spend thirty minutes outside walking around the campus by ourselves, just thinking about our favorite thirty-five words that could paint a picture of where we were going and who we, as a company, wanted to be in five years' time.

We all knew we were close to arriving at something special and somewhat permanent: our company vision. Upon our return, I was the brave one and volunteered to go first. I made a statement with nine words. The facilitator wrote them on the board and asked everyone what they thought. Everyone looked at each other and said, "That's it – done!" The combination of the positive exercise and the power walk had inspired me to find a creative solution – an inspiring phrase that captured our company's vision.

The facilitator spent some time challenging us and pushing back on our new vision statement to ensure it was solid. After some discussion, we decided to leave it unchanged and still – to this day – it is helping the company's employees align with a common purpose.

OUTDOOR LESSON

In the early days of our team-building company, we were privileged to work with a small team of twelve managers from one of the largest and most successful software companies in Seattle, Washington.

We received a last-minute call at our headquarters in Park City, Utah, from a VP who had seen our brochure in the hotel during one of their meeting breaks. The phone call went something like this: "Hey, I know this is crazy-late, but any chance you could do an activity for our team tonight?"

Given that it was 12:15 in the afternoon my response was a bit guarded: "We would love to, but before I say yes, can I learn a little bit about your team and what you are trying to accomplish?"

The following story will give you some insight into why this adventure makes it into our chapter on creativity. I had a great conversation with the team leader and could tell we had a connection. He mentioned that his team was stuck on finding some business solutions for a big product launch. They needed workable ideas by the end of their retreat. I asked what else they had been doing while in Park City, and he stated that they had been hunkered down in their meeting room intensely trying to work on the business solutions.

As an aside, we often wonder why so many teams come to Park City to wonder at the beauty of the Wasatch Mountains and then spend their time in a hotel conference room instead of the great outdoors. Mother Nature can surely help to unlock the creative solutions that sit inside your team's minds and simply need to be released.

I also learned that even though the team leader wanted to do an early-evening activity, we needed to finish in time for an expensive dinner reservation at a brewpub on Main Street.

I ended the call by saying, "Let me get with my team and brainstorm some ideas for a fun adventure, and we'll meet your team in your hotel lobby at 5:30 tonight. And please make sure your team is dressed appropriately for winter weather with snow in the forecast."

He replied, "That's awesome, but what should I expect for the cost?"

Being a long-time sales guy, I quoted a standard price range for most of our adventures. I added that since this event was fully customized for his team, he could pay us whatever he felt was fair based on the value we brought to his team.

He replied "Sweet. I like the way you roll. See you at 5:30."

As soon as I hung up the phone, I rounded up my team of guides and asked if they were busy tonight, because we had some fun work to do. One of our core values at Park City Teamworks is "Work hard and play hard." Our team believes the more you can blur the distinction between work and play, then the more passion the team can bring to high performance. Now it was our time to perform.

I started the brainstorming session with some game rules:

1. We had already agreed to do the event, so failure was not an option.
2. We only had thirty minutes to come up with a top-shelf idea that we'd be proud to deliver.
3. There were no bad ideas without someone having a better idea. Let's storm!

Our head guide kicked off the session with, "Let me start by saying that you are nuts, and that's why we love you." We all laughed and began a high-energy, highly creative session.

The creative solution was to take our Alpine Discovery mountain adventure to Main Street and add a silver mining theme. This was the birth of one of our more popular adventures: Explore Park City.

In essence, we took seven of our proven team-building stations from the mountain and placed them throughout historic Main Street at the mining-related parks, statues, and museums. Cool idea, and now we needed to move fast to execute on the idea. We "divided and conquered" by getting permission from Town Hall and setting GPS coordinates for all seven sites. Boom! By 4:00 p.m., our team was ready to rock and roll.

Our two teams met in the hotel lobby, and we made an instant connection. They were ready for an adventure after being caged inside all day, and Mother Nature added her special touch with the famous Utah "greatest snow on earth."

We had a magical night together as we explored Park City while challenging the group's three small teams to be creative, collaborative, and competitive as they solved puzzles, overcame obstacles, and racked up points at the seven stations. The adventure ended at the brewpub, just in time for dinner in the reserved private room where we led a debrief with the three teams.

As you may realize by now, we end all of our adventures with a debrief of lessons learned. We use our simple ART acronym: Adventure (a journey to the unknown), Reflection (zoom out and look back at lessons learned), and Transfer (take the outdoor lessons back to the workplace). We believe this is our company's greatest strength and where we bring the most value to our clients' journey to the top. This snowy night was no exception.

As one of the team guides that night, I had witnessed an extremely creative solution to one of our more popular challenges named High Camp. It is designed to simulate the epic adventure high on Mount Everest from the book *Into Thin Air* by Jon Krakauer. In this riveting book, Krakauer relates the true story about a number of climbing teams returning to the South Col exhausted, disoriented, and on the edge of death, desperate to find the safety of their tents.

Our challenge is designed to be far from the dangers at the top of the world, however, it simulates a common team challenge – communication. The team is faced with the survival challenge of putting up a technical tent while half of the team members are "snowblind" and the other half are "frostbitten." The "frostbitten" members cannot touch the tent, and the "snowblind" members cannot see the tent. Hence, the necessary communication between team members.

I have facilitated our High Camp challenge hundreds of times with teams from around the world, and it is truly amazing how poorly adult professionals perform at this challenge. We have seen it all including work colleagues ripping off their blindfolds and yelling, "You wear the damn thing, and I will tell you what to do!" Often, even simulated stress can truly bring out the worst in leaders.

This team was different. Highly intelligent, highly collaborative, and highly creative. As we began our ART debrief session during dinner, I reflected back on my team's performance at High Camp. The team began the challenge by asking good questions and probing for good solutions. One of the quiet engineers named Will stood up and said, "Guys, this is a simple robotics exercise."

"What are you thinking?" a teammate asked.

"Simple. We take the folks who have the most tent-building experience and make them 'frostbitten,' then we take the other two people who have less experience and make them 'snowblind.' Next, the folks who can see stand behind the blindfolded folks and direct all their movements. You know, just binary communication only."

After a bit more explaining, the team was all in. A challenge that takes an average of twenty-seven minutes was conquered in nine minutes. This team still holds the record.

I finished telling this amazing story during the debrief, and the entire group started cheering and high fiving each other in celebration. After summarizing that particular *Adventure*, I asked the team to *Reflect* and talk about any lessons that could be *Transferred* back to the workplace.

The senior leader stood and said, "The key learning for me – and what I challenge all of us to take back to our morning meeting – is simple. We are all super smart and super creative. We just have to believe in ourselves, and the solutions will come. Let's enjoy the rest of the evening and trust that our team will get unstuck tomorrow morning and find the best possible solution. Now who's with me on this?"

You can imagine the team's exuberant response. I ended our debrief and time together by following the high energy with, "Thank you for the adventure together tonight. Now, go forward and find the solutions that surely sit within your collective genius."

The next afternoon, I got a follow-up call from the VP as he was on his way to the airport. He thanked me for the adventure and told me his team did, in fact, come up with some great solutions while still at the brewpub after we left. He credited our team for helping to get his team unstuck, adding that the best, most creative solution could be worth millions of dollars. He paid more than a fair price for our services and gave our guides a healthy tip.

It was a memorable event and a reminder of the value our small outdoor leadership company provides to some of the largest companies in the world. The story didn't end that snowy winter night. I got a call six months later from my new VP friend. He asked if we could come to Seattle to provide an adventure for the team responsible for the new product launch. I asked him what he wanted to accomplish.

"Well, to start, the adventure will be for the entire launch team of 250 people," he said.

I almost dropped the phone but decided to try to play it cool by continuing my interview. Our team pulled off another amazing event in a thick fir forest along Puget Sound. A great lesson in the power of team creativity from both sides of the isle.

HOMEWORK/TEAM TALK

Most of the winning teams we have worked with over the years have the internal strength to find creative solutions to all the challenges they face. It starts with the team leader building an environment that nurtures creativity. Here are some things you can work on.

1. As a leader and as a team, constantly challenge yourselves to get better at the five things that release team creativity:
   a. Have a strong team vision for growth.
   b. Remember the dance of reflection.
   c. Nurture caring and respect of diversity.

d. Have positivity to open your minds.

e. Nurture the desire to learn and elevate quality.

2. Design a creative space for your team gatherings:

   a. Meet outdoors.

   b. Gather in circles.

   c. Use artwork to open the mind.

   d. Use toys like Legos to build on an idea.

   e. Use a community blackboard to capture random ideas.

3. Incorporate meditation, walking, or fluid movements before or during your session to promote a more expansive thought process and facilitate creativity. Here are just a few ideas:

   a. Meditation

   b. Hula hooping

   c. Tai Chi

   d. Lego building

   e. Painting

4. Use a new technique for your next brainstorming workshop such as the brain writing concept described earlier. Alternatively, try using sticky notes to spark the creative process. Here's how it works:

   a. All team members get their own pad of sticky notes.

   b. The facilitator writes down the problem statement for all to see and asks for a minimum of ten specific and actionable solutions to the problem.

   c. Everyone writes down one idea per sticky note. It is a silent exercise for five to ten minutes.

   d. The facilitator gathers the sticky notes and randomly sticks all the ideas on a wall for all to see.

   e. Next, the group breaks into small teams of two or three people and works together on five new ideas using all the notes on the wall to spark creative ideas. This may take a bit longer:

about fifteen minutes. This process will surely elevate your team's creativity by engaging your introverts, generating a large number of ideas, and allowing team members to build on each other's ideas.

5. Have the courage to lead those uncomfortable and revealing conversations to cultivate an environment of psychological safety. Here are some suggestions:

    a. Sit down with your team and ask each member to share thoughts to make sure they are supporting one another.

    b. Individuals need to ask themselves: What do I need to feel psychologically safe? How can I help the organization give me that? How can I make it apparent when I don't feel safe, so I can be helped?

If you feel like your team is truly stuck and the magnitude of the project allows for the budget, then consider hiring a professional facilitator who specializes in creativity or an adventure company that uses the great outdoors to spark fresh, new ideas.

CHAPTER 7

COURAGE SUMMIT – Overcome Adversity and Challenge the Status Quo

THE TOP-PERFORMING TEAMS we have witnessed over the years have the courage to share leadership, overcome adversity, and take calculated risks. In our data of more than 300 Alpine Discovery adventure races, 42 percent of the winning teams had the courage to tackle the most difficult challenge first. All the participating teams have time at the start of the race to prepare a "plan of attack." The courageous teams agree to go for High Camp as their first challenge. High Camp is always designed to be the highest and farthest station from Base Camp. It is also the camp with the most difficult team challenge. Rightfully so, it earns the highest reward in revenue (points) earned.

The second most successful strategy for winning teams is to target the easiest challenge closest to Base Camp. These teams win 23 percent of the time. These teams figure they should go for the "easy money" and build confidence and energy from the start. Certainly not courageous but a solid, intelligent strategy.

What is it about the courageous teams that take the calculated risk to go for the top right out of the gate that makes them almost twice as successful as the second most successful strategy? We will explore courage in more detail throughout this summit.

THE 7 SUMMITS OF WINNING TEAMS
Winning teams are, have, or use:

CHIEF	=	Served by a 4S Leader
CHEMISTRY	=	Diversity of Thought and Complementary Skills
COMPASS	=	Common Purpose, Alignment, and Destination
CENTERED	=	Balance of Competition and Collaboration
COMMUNITY	=	Trust, Care, and Share
CREATIVITY	=	Solutions from Within
COURAGE	=	**Overcome Adversity and Challenge the Status Quo**

First, let's look at some different definitions of courage, both traditional and contemporary. Traditional dictionary definitions typically include concepts such as strength and perseverance despite danger or difficulty. This ties well to my passion for adventure. Pushing your body, mind, and spirit beyond what you thought was possible certainly takes courage.

Let's look at a more modern definition. On her website, author Brene Brown writes that associating courage with heroic deeds fails to take into consideration the inner strength required to speak honestly and openly. She refers to speaking from your heart as *ordinary courage.*

We like this definition, because it is less masculine and looks inward rather than outward at facing danger. It is more hopeful than fearful. One is not more correct than the other, but in this summit we are looking at courage in relationship to teams, not individuals.

We did find another definition that is quite powerful from the Native American Lakota people. Courage is part of their Four Virtues along with generosity, respect, and wisdom. The virtues tie to their medicine wheel and have been used for thousands of years to develop their youth to become adults. In Lakota, courage or bravery is the attribute that is needed to take care of others, for example, facing a difficult challenge or situation for the sake of others.

I really like this definition, because it is outward facing and more about using your gift of courage for the benefit of others. It feels like it connects better to our core value of team courage.

In his book *Return on Courage: A Business Playbook for Courageous Change*, author Ryan Berman explores the need for courage in today's business world. He states that 52 percent of the *Fortune* 500 companies from the year 2000 are no longer in business. Shocking. It speaks to the magnitude and frequency of change found in the modern marketplace. Business teams need to be brave and face their changing landscape head on, be willing to adapt, and courageously plow forward.

He defines *knowledge* as the clarity collected through education and experience. *Faith* is the belief that success will be found even before all the answers are proven. And he defines *action* as fighting off the fear of change, leaning in, and taking the first bold step.

We agree that team courage is about being smart and mitigating the known risk, but then you need to either individually or collectively stick your neck out before it is safe. We believe that individual and team growth truly only takes place outside of our comfort zones. Courage is about leaving the safety of home and exploring beyond our comfort. History has shown that true greatness often lies on the outer fringes of the ordinary.

In our research on courage, we found dozens of articles and books on individual leadership courage, but few are focused on team courage. To understand the impact of ignoring insecurity in the workplace, it is helpful to understand a bit about the psychology of fear. According to Dr. Margie Warrell, an author and global authority on leading with courage, if people feel insecure they can overestimate the risks, underestimate themselves, and play it safe. While this can temporarily provide the illusion of safety, it generally makes people (and organizations) feel less secure in the long term.

It becomes clear that, left unchecked, a culture of fear will leave your employees distracted and underperforming and will leave your organization stagnating instead of courageously pursuing creativity and innovation.

There is no doubt that team courage begins with the leader. If you are feeling your team's culture is constraining its courage, consider the following strategies prescribed by Dr. Warrell to help your team members take brave actions. (Learn more at www.MargieWarrell.com.)

1. Activate the "rally effect" to pull people into a shared mission-critical fight.
2. Work to get it right versus being right.
3. Encourage "loyal dissenters."
4. Listen for unspoken fears – and speak to them.
5. Embolden people to play to win.
6. Destigmatize failure.
7. Operate from a "don't know mind."

Core to these steps is cultivating a safe team culture where there is psychological safety to take risks. To inspire innovation, a skilled leader encourages strategic risk-taking and reframes early failures into lessons learned. This removes the fear of failure and makes it a safe place to push the boundaries of conventional thinking.

One of our favorite illustrations of creating a safe culture comes from the popular TV series, *Ted Lasso*. New in his role as coach of a soccer team – and with a great deal to learn about the sport – Ted asks Nate, the underappreciated equipment manager, for his ideas to improve team performance. Nobody realized that Nate has some brilliant ideas about how to coach the team. When Nate gets up the courage to tell Ted his ideas, Ted listens, values his opinion, and then incorporates his ideas. What's more, when Ted is asked by the media who developed one specific play in particular, he gives Nate the credit.

Seeking out team members' opinions and then actively using their suggestions creates psychological safety: the belief you can share ideas, disagree, and ask questions of your team without fear that you will be singled out, put down, or otherwise embarrassed.

Our work with teams also reveals that leaders who seek to cultivate courage must also muster the courage to walk the talk themselves. This means leading with the right tension – acting with humility and recognizing their own vulnerabilities – while at the same time leading with confidence that the team goals are achievable.

Dr. Warrell describes leaders as "emotional barometers of their team's feelings," because they provide cues to employees on how to respond and behave. If leaders show up anxious, the team will adopt this anxiety. Leaders should take care to ground themselves, so they show up in control of themselves. When the team sees their leader is in control of herself/himself, they will feel more confident to be braver.

CARABINER KEY POINT:

It is clear from witnessing business teams that show a
high level of courage that the qualities of team courage are both contagious and compounding.

Courage is surprisingly contagious! Once teammates see that courage is encouraged and rewarded within the team, then they feel motivated to step up and be bolder themselves. Courage also appears to build on itself like compound interest, and smaller acts of courage grow and become more significant with each experience.

The following stories from both business and adventure illustrate the need for courage in winning teams.

INDOOR LESSON

In the fall of 1999, my wife and I filed our articles of incorporation in the state of Utah for Wasatch Adventure Consultants LLC – an outdoor leadership company focused on business teams (later rebranded as Park City Teamworks). We formed the company swiftly after just thirty days of pounding out a business plan, but the seeds were planted many years earlier. This story is founded on business courage and following your passion.

The premise for the business plan was simple: a thoughtful blend of indoor leadership lessons and outdoor business adventures. Our motto, "Work hard and play hard," speaks to our core belief that work should be attacked with the same passion as play. We also believe we are much stronger together than we are apart. And that's why high-performing, winning teams are critical to helping a business get to the top.

The concept of blending business and adventure began when I was in the fourth grade. I grew up in a family of five with a single mom. We were poor financially, yet rich with love. In 1974, we moved from California to Connecticut to be near my mother's family. In Oakland, we had attended a small Catholic school where we wore uniforms. On our first day of public school in Connecticut, we were excited to be able to dress in clothes of our choice.

Unfortunately, that excitement didn't last long for me. I came home that first day in tears and told my mother that I needed a job, so I could buy my own clothes. Sure enough, the new kid got picked on by the cool kids, because my hand-me-down jeans had patches on both knees.

That weekend I signed up for two paper routes, morning and afternoon, and my career as an entrepreneur began. I was bound and determined to be the best paperboy in town. This job combined two of my passions – bike riding and throwing. More importantly, I began buying my own clothes at age eleven.

That same year, my Cub Scouts leader sponsored me to attend a two-week summer camp in Maine called Outward Bound. I was a shy kid growing up in my older brother's shadow, and more significantly, I had been bullied for much of my early life. It started in kindergarten when my mom dropped me off with a kiss and told me she loved me. I had no idea what was in store for me that first day. See, I was small for my age, had a patch on my left eye for a condition called lazy eye, and wore steel braces on both legs for severely ducked feet. A sight to see, for sure.

When my mom got home from work, she found me crying in my room. She didn't have to ask how my first day of school went, so she spun one of her magical lessons that has stuck with me my whole life: "Sticks and stones may break your bones, but words can never hurt you." To this day, I have no time or place for bullies in my life.

Outward Bound has built a world-class brand on changing kids' and young adults' lives for the better. I am a proud alumnus and thankful recipient of a changed life.

The first life lesson Outward Bound taught me was the power of Mother Nature and her ability to heal and nurture. For two weeks we learned all the skills to survive in the wilderness – building a proper shelter, starting a fire from scratch, purifying water, hunting, and gathering food. At my core, it changed my belief in myself. The knowledge that I could be dropped off anywhere in the world and I possessed the skills to survive changed my life. It also built the foundation for connecting the outdoors to leadership training.

I share some of my background not so you can feel sorry for me. Just the opposite. I tell it to show that we all have the power to be courageous deep within ourselves. Society has robbed most of us from tapping into our innate courage by teaching fear and aversion to risk. This allows most of us to take the safe path in life, yet the truth shows us that greatness lies outside the boundaries of our comfort zone. Launching a new business from scratch has clearly been the single most courageous act of my life. My hope is that some of my lessons can spark courage within you.

Before starting my entrepreneurial adventure, I was considered a young executive with a bright future. Our company's sales team was enjoying much success and coming off two consecutive years of double-digit growth. Our board of directors was entertaining the possibility of going public, and we were interviewing prospective investment banking firms to lead our initial public offering (IPO). It was an exciting time to be part of the executive team.

After one of our trips to Wall Street, our company president called me into his office. He told me one of the firms had recommended our company hire a new VP of sales with more years of experience than me and with experience leading a $500 million public company. This would help us attract an elevated IPO that would be good for both me and the company. I sat there in shock and silence, as this was a massive gut punch. He continued his sales pitch by adding that this demotion would be a positive step for my young career, as I would get to learn under this great new sales leader.

After much soul searching and long nights talking it over with my wife, I decided to be a good soldier and see how working for my new boss would turn out. I had poured my heart and soul into building a great sales team, so deep down I knew my days at this company were numbered. I knew I could never give the same level of passion to a company and a mentor who had broken my trust.

At the time, I was commuting from Utah to Connecticut two weeks a month and could often be found on the red-eye flight to the John F. Kennedy International Airport on Sunday nights. On my own time, I began to spark my entrepreneurial fire by researching ideas for my own business. I began with the concept of investing in a franchise, but I simply couldn't center the idea of giving someone $150,000 just for a proven toolkit to build a business that was someone else's dream.

Consistently, I kept coming back to the idea of taking my hard-earned $150,000 and investing in my own dream. That all sounded great, but exactly what was that dream and how could I make a living following my passion? I have learned that if you keep asking your mind and praying to God for guidance, then you will eventually find your answer. And when I kept asking the core question – *What was I put on this earth to be and do better than anyone else?* – I kept coming back to running a team-building business that combined indoor leadership with outdoor adventures.

When I inherited that company's sales force, we had a traditional, all-male culture with internal competition being the overriding driver. Our quarterly sales meetings often included fishing or golf outings. We called them team-building events, but they were far from it with only a few winners and many losers. As the new leader, I wanted to change the culture from win-loss to win-win.

We began to hire corporate team-building companies from around the country to lead events for our quarterly sales meetings. The events were a welcome change and certainly promoted team-building concepts, but it was clear something was missing – there was no connection between the adventure and our business. The consultants weren't helping us to identify and apply any insights we experienced in the adventures, so we could truly become a better, higher-performing team at work.

After each event, I began running our own debrief sessions to tie the lessons from the day back to actionable lessons for our sales team. I realized this would be the "secret sauce" for my new business.

Meanwhile, that company completed a national search for a new VP and hired my new boss in January. He was a seasoned professional with experience running a $500 million business, however, he had no experience in our industry. After six months, it became painfully clear that he was not elevating my career, rather, I was training him on how to do his job. It was time to make a change, but this type of change would require a massive amount of courage.

Countless successful business folks have stood at this fork in the road. The road to the left is the easy choice – smooth and comfortable. Remain at the company, keep the safety of a weekly paycheck, and be patient with the hope things may get better. The road to the right is the courageous choice – rocky and challenging. Resign from the company, and take the high risk of starting your own business. Now more two decades later, having made that difficult choice, I know why most folks make the safe choice.

Taking a giant leap is scary and takes a tremendous amount of courage. I knew an objective tool could help me make the right decision. Early in my career at a management training class I learned about the Franklin T-Test – a simple tool Benjamin Franklin used to help him make difficult decisions. Whenever you need to make a challenging decision, I encourage you to use the Franklin T-Test. As an example, I will share the T-Test I used to make the most difficult decision of my career.

FRANKLIN T-TEST

Question: Should I leave the comfort of my executive income for the high risk and potential reward of starting my own company?

POSITIVES	NEGATIVES
Be happy	Not happy
Follow my dream	Loss of guaranteed annual income
More quality time with my family	Miss IPO stock sale
Scratch my entrepreneurial itch	Loss of security
Do what I do best	No family health insurance
Help hundreds of teams	Leave a great team
Increase income in two-to-three years	Place our dream house on hold
Less travel	Spend life savings
Join community leadership	Negotiate non-compete agreement
Take ownership of my career	
Get back to peak fitness	

Answer: The positives outweigh the negatives. See if my wife will support this decision. Seek advice from my personal council.

It is worth noting that the Franklin T-Test does not place any weight on any one row, as its beauty is found in its simplicity. I did actually place some weight based on my highest values of happiness and family. Most of the negatives were driven by money, and this is a lower personal value for me.

Courage is often defined by facing your fears and taking risks. As business leaders we learn to mitigate the risks through rigorous analysis. We use history, data, and assumptions to make the most thoughtful decisions with the least amount of risk. And experienced leaders learn that many of the assumptions will be wrong, so success requires the ability to pivot quickly to correct the course.

The following lessons are some steps that I took to mitigate some of the risks before making my courageous decision. I hope you find them helpful:

- *Step 1: Seek support from your spouse* – The full, unwavering support from your loved ones is paramount to the success of any new business venture.
- *Step 2: Seek advice from your personal council* – If you don't already have a handful of friends, family, or mentors you can turn to for honest advice, then begin by establishing these relationships prior to taking the leap.
- *Step 3: Write an executive summary business plan* – Your new business is just a wild, far-fetched idea until you go through the discipline of writing a formal business plan. (Templates are available online.)
- *Step 4: Get your finances in order* – We have all seen data showing that the number-one cause of failure in the start-up phase is undercapitalization. Don't even think about launching a new business without being able to cover six months of personal expenses. Loans from family, home equity, and credit cards were not off limits in my case.

- ***Step 5: Build local business partnerships*** – This is a key step that can be overlooked, yet most successful businesses require B2B partnerships, either formal or informal. We made these visits our first priority.
- ***Step 6: Seek advice to establish a legal entity*** – This step can often be overlooked. However, it must be one of the first investments. As an adventure company, our selection of a limited liability company (LLC) was both straightforward and essential.
- ***Step 7: Hire service providers for website and logo design*** – This is not the place to cut corners. You only get one chance to make a first impression. Make it count.

Our story was much more than my personal and family entrepreneurial journey. Like most successful stories, it included the courage and contributions from a team. And in many ways the courage that was required to join our team in the early stages far exceeded my personal leap of faith.

Like many founders, for years I had a framed copy of the first check ever made out to Wasatch Adventure Consultants above my desk. We were blessed to earn the business of a local automotive safety company in Utah. A group of global managers signed up to experience our Park City Autobahn event, which was an exhilarating 75-mph trip down the actual Olympic bobsled track. We were the first company to rent the facility for corporate events that connected the adventure of a lifetime, followed by a celebration at the Olympic Lodge. The experience is now open to the public thanks in part to our vision.

That opening night, I invited a handful of friends to facilitate the event. We held a briefing prior to the event, and I passed along my vision for the new company: "The lines between work and play need to be blurred, so business teams can attack their work with the same passion as they play." The night was a huge success, and our venture was off and running like a bobsled down the icy track.

In the following months, a handful of my associates from the opening night told me they caught the vision and asked how they could be more involved. Each of these friends left successful careers to join our young startup, and to this day, I remain humbled and grateful for the extreme courage they showed. A special thanks to all the Park City Teamworks guides/facilitators who kept our clients safe and enriched my life.

Our story of business courage is much more than just taking personal risk. Courage is about believing in yourself, following your dreams, and shouting your vision from the tallest mountaintop, so more courageous leaders can join your team and help to make it a success.

OUTDOOR LESSON

A few years ago, an international investment firm based in New York City hired Park City Teamworks to work with a group of the company's future leaders. We worked directly with the VP of talent to add an indoor workshop prior to their summertime outdoor adventure. We are always excited to get this level of commitment from our clients, because we know from experience that it increases the depth of learning from our engagement.

We chose to use the StrengthsFinder 2.0 book in the workshop and instructed the twenty-five participants to take the online assessment prior to the workshop. We then built a spreadsheet of all the profiles including the two executives. We color-coded the spreadsheet with the four main StrengthsFinder themes – Striving, Relating, Impacting, and Thinking – and then inserted each guest's five core strengths. This allowed the group to quickly get a powerful visual representation of how diverse they may or may not be.

The workshop was scheduled for two hours and was designed to hit the highlights of the StrengthsFinder book and assessment tool. The morning session went quite well with full engagement from the participants.

We chose a great setting for the workshop and adventure: Soldier Hollow in Utah. It was the 2002 Olympic Nordic venue, sits at the foot of Mount Timpanogos, and has a restored old timber lodge we could use for Base Camp. You could sense the anxiety level rise during lunch as we briefed the group on the adventure race we had in store for them in the afternoon.

Prior to the event, we worked with HR to create four cross-functional teams based on each participant's geography, functional area, and strengths. We also gave each team member a colored bandana to wear as a quick visual key to identify their main strength theme.

I was assigned to Team 2, because it included the VP of talent named Victoria, and we had already built a relationship during the pre-work for the event. She was originally from Australia and had great energy. She had worked her way up the organization with both smarts and people skills.

We gathered our small team for the mandatory fifteen-minute strategic planning session. In this adventure race each team must pick a strategy to complete the seven Camps (stations) before the cutoff time of 4:00 p.m. When we design a course, we assign a point value to each Camp based on the distance of travel and the difficulty of the team-building challenge. High Camp is always the highest value but comes with the greatest risks.

High Camp at Soldier Hollow lived up to its name. It was located high on the mountainside with a massive rock outcropping named Indian Rock. For the challenge, we set up a mountain rescue scenario that would require the team to assemble a rescue stretcher and then all safely rappel down a sixty-foot overhanging cliff. A full-on adventure for any team.

Victoria began our planning session by asking all the right questions: "What is our collective goal?" The answer was clear: "We want to win!" She then asked, "Does anyone have adventure skills or survival experience?" Check, Jake was an Army Ranger commander.

"Jake, are you comfortable leading us?" she asked.

"Yes, ma'am."

Jake began his leadership reign by asking the team members if they would be comfortable focusing on the target-rich High Camp first. He explained that by taking the high ground first, we could then see the entire course layout and work our way down the hill to Base Camp, giving our team the best chance to win.

The team had full buy-in, and everyone supported Jake's plan. As I looked into the eyes of each team member, I found one reluctant participant: Victoria. We traded a quick nod, as she was not yet willing to reveal her hesitancy for High Camp's challenge. I suspected she didn't like the idea of the rope challenge due to a fear of heights, as this was a common fear for many of our guests.

Our team set off on our journey to High Camp, and I told them it would be a minimum of a thirty-minute, uphill struggle. The hike wasn't easy for anyone, but it was obvious that Victoria was struggling the most. The team dynamic was solid, as they were supportive yet fully understood that "we are only as strong as our weakest link."

We were making slow but steady progress until suddenly Victoria went down with a scream. She had been pressing uphill too hard and had twisted her ankle on a loose rock. We all gathered around her as I assessed the ankle injury. Thankfully, it appeared to be a mild sprain, so we put a brace on her ankle, which would allow her to walk to safety.

I told the team that my recommendation would be to radio Base Camp and have an ATV come out and take Victoria back to an emergency medical technician at the lodge. A quick response from one of her teammates was that if Victoria had to go back, then we all had to go back. A really cool statement that likely spoke to the leadership trust she had earned. Victoria asked me if she could continue on the bad ankle. I responded, "Not if you are planning to walk, but the rules allow you to be carried."

Her team jumped at the opportunity to make a stretcher out of a tarp and two tree limbs. It helps to have an Army Ranger in charge. We were two-thirds up the climb, and the team performed the final third in flying colors. Their spirits were elevated, and we arrived at High Camp. Team adversity is often the key ingredient in building mettle for future success. This team was no exception.

The team listened to the two professional climbing guides as they explained the challenge of getting the entire team down the rock face including a rescue stretcher used by rescue teams in a real mountain retrieval. Jake began by asking everyone how comfortable they were with heights and whether anyone had ever rappelled before. He also proclaimed that we had the perfect volunteer for the stretcher: Victoria.

I was placing an ice pack on Victoria's ankle when this discussion was going on, and I could feel her shaking. I asked quietly if she was ok. She replied that she was deathly afraid of abseiling. This is the Australian term for rappelling, but I had never heard it before. I leaned in closer and asked for clarification. She blurted out, "I will not be abseiling or bloody rappelling or whatever you Americans call it!" The entire team heard this and came over to comfort her.

We were able to provide comfort to Victoria through the team, the guides, and the team leader Jake. The combined trust gave Victoria the strength to agree to be lowered down a sixty-foot cliff without any personal control. And we all know how hard it is for any leader to give up control. She showed an incredible amount of courage by showing her team it was ok to be vulnerable, by giving her team the highest level of trust, and by overcoming a life-long fear of heights.

When she safely arrived at the base of the rock cliff with the entire team cheering, she wiped away tears and said, "If I can do this, then I can do anything." A powerful statement from a courageous leader. The team fought through adversity, rallied around their leader, and found the inner strength to finish the adventure with elevated performance.

Prior to our post-event debrief, I asked Victoria for permission to share her story with the entire work group, because there was much to be learned by her leadership. She agreed and together we highlighted the experience and key learnings. The lessons included taking risks, overcoming fear, fighting through adversity, trusting your team, and leadership vulnerability.

This is the magic of business adventures – the fact that four hours in the mountains can drive home such rich learnings that everyone can take back to their work to become better leaders and a high-performing team.

The team's plan to be courageous and go for High Camp first was rewarded. Appropriate for her name, Victoria's team was empowered to finish the adventure in victory. In our twenty years of experience, we have found that the teams combining courage and smarts most often win in both adventure and business.

HOMEWORK/TEAM TALK

We believe team courage is a learned behavior through practice and can be contagious within the team. As teammates witness other leaders stepping up, they are encouraged to do the same – this time and next time. And through encouragement and practice, they build their trust and confidence to become a courageous team.

Here are some steps you can take to embolden each team member to dare to do their best work:

1. Start at the top by being a courageous leader. When you role-model humility about what you don't know, you make it safer for your team to let go of their own fears and lean into brave actions and inspired ideas.

2. Take the stigma out of failure. Lead robust discussions about early failures and important lessons learned from them as part of the regular team conversation. Create psychological safety to encourage team members to be bold and know they will be ok when they take

risks. The important thing is how many times your team gets back up rather than how many times it falls.

3. Listen for unspoken fears and draw them out into the open. Remote work has left many employees feeling disconnected and isolated. Make it a regular practice to check in with each team member and really listen to how they are doing. Speaking aloud unspoken fears will help to alleviate them and help the team refocus on the challenges at hand. Regularly ask your team members:

    a. What's the greatest challenge on your plate?

    b. What can I do to support you now?

    c. What obstacles are keeping you from moving forward?

4. Embolden people to perform at their best by leaning into their strengths. People rise to the level of expectations others have of them. If you micromanage your team, you convey lack of confidence. To embolden your team to reach their full potential look for opportunities to:

    a. Delegate decision making.

    b. Let them know you have their back.

    c. Tell them it's ok to fail when it is.

5. Schedule a Fear Workshop with your team by being vulnerable and identifying fears. Winning teams do not avoid their fears but instead they face them head-on.

    a. Break the workshop into three sections: identify your personal fears, identify your team fears, and identify your customer/ stakeholder fears.

    b. Once identified, spend some time exploring solutions to the fears. Start by shrinking the big intimidating fears into manageable smaller ones. Like successful mountain climbers, break the fear of climbing the entire mountain into smaller camps that can be tackled in one-day climbs.

c. Test your best solutions and spend time reflecting on how to make the ideas even better. Challenge everyone to have the team courage to commit to helping each other improve individually and collectively.

Winning teams have the courage to overcome adversity and face their collective fears along with the trust to work together to conquer them. Greatness is found outside the safety of comfort zones.

The global COVID-19 pandemic surely changed the way we operate as work teams. We will explore some of those challenges in the following Bonus Summit. Today, maybe more than ever, team courage is paramount in our quest for the top.

CHAPTER 8

BONUS SUMMIT – How to Win Now and in the Future with Hybrid Teams

IN 2022 PARK CITY TEAMWORKS began a research project to identify the post-pandemic changes to the American workplace and, specifically, the effect on work teams. We felt this Bonus Chapter was essential to validate the twenty-plus years of research that forged the 7 Summits. Specifically, do the tried-and-true lessons from our list of 7 Summits of Winning Teams still hold true for the great number of new hybrid teams? A critical question indeed.

On the good news front, we have not been short on research material. Hardly a day goes by where our daily news feeds don't have at least a few relevant articles on hybrid teams and remote work. The bad news is that the research and data are actually quite varied, and the future of the American workforce is unclear to many experts.

It is clear that the pandemic accelerated the rate and magnitude of changes in the way we work. All nonessential employers were forced to send their employees home to work remotely. Many workers found remote work to be a blessing by gaining both freedom and time. Most companies found that production rates from remote workers remained high. Once mask-wearing policies were lifted, companies opened their office doors and asked employees to return. On whole, as we write this chapter, it is fair to say that most employees are pushing back on return-to-office mandates.

Gallup's measurement of working U.S. adults shows that millennials – those born between 1980 and 1996 – make up 38 percent of the workforce. It's estimated that this number will grow to 75 percent by the year 2025. Unfortunately, millennials have a reputation for being flight risks. If that reputation is true, this makes it vital for organizations to understand how to engage and retain these employees. What does it take for a company to keep the good people around?

Companies will have to attract and retain the best talent to win in the hybrid workplace. To do so, they'll have to adapt to the wants and needs of their employees and keep them engaged. Employees will not stick around the modern workplace because of things like ping pong tables and free espresso. Gallup finds that an informal work environment is the least essential job factor among millennial job seekers. Just 15 percent of millennials state that this job factor is extremely important to them when applying for a job.

In the following paragraphs, we will address the most pressing questions as they relate to the hybrid workforce and winning teams. We will do our best to interpret the conflicting data and draw conclusions based on our significant experience working with business teams for more than twenty years. We think you will hear a common theme from a previous chapter – the best answers often lie in the middle.

INTRO QUESTION

In the coming years, where will work teams
land on the issue of remote work?

It is clear that the pandemic accelerated the rate of change toward remote work. It is also likely that the workplace has changed for good. For many, it has changed for the better. The five-day/eight-hour work week and long commutes to the office have been with us for decades, with roots in the Industrial Revolution. Change needed to happen.

Employees have had time to reflect on what is important to them, and turnover rates of approximately 65 percent reflect the desire for new models of work. The key demands include expanded benefits, compensation, and flexibility. Navigating the tension between corporate control and employee flexibility will be a major theme for leaders going forward.

We believe that as we settle into the new normal, hybrid teams will be prevalent at the majority of companies. In fact, over the past few decades, the workplace has become a global marketplace. And as companies have become more international, so have their work teams. These global teams have paved the way for the current hybrid teams.

The future will most likely have a distributed workforce. While many executives are excited to return their organization to a 100 percent in-person environment, this type of workplace is no longer the norm. Plus, many talented, younger employees would not even consider working for a company with a strict back-to-office policy.

Many occupations will remain remote and function at a high level. Other roles will be hybrid with employees balancing a combination of remote work and in-office time.

Companies that invested millions of dollars into building an amazing headquarters on a sprawling campus are certainly going to ask workers to come back to the office multiple days of the week, because those companies must have a strong belief in collaboration and culture to make such investments in their headquarters.

At the time of this writing, we have a strong economy and high levels of employment, so all the leverage appears to be with workers. That means leaders need to be open and flexible with their policies if they want to keep their talent. However, the economy will shift at some point, and the leverage will go back to employers and likely to more traditional work policies. We also believe humans are by nature social beings who thrive in teams and tribes. Winning hybrid teams will find the best remote collaboration tools and also find ways to maximize quality time with their teammates.

CHIEF QUESTIONS
How will 4S Leaders have to adapt to effectively manage their new hybrid teams?

By design, 4S Leaders are better at adapting to change by being less rigid and open to new ideas by choosing the blended leadership styles: Shared, Servant, Situational, and Strength-based. For many, the new hybrid "situation" will ask them to adapt to the changing workforce preference for location and schedule flexibility. Leaders who take the opportunity to transform how work is accomplished can help the organization drive growth, mitigate environmental risks, and attract and retain top talent. This transformation includes figuring out the hybrid model that works best for their organization as well as updating practices and policies that support the model.

Leaders will need to navigate concerns about hybrid work including eroding culture and the impact on mentoring, innovation, and inclusiveness between remote and in-office team members. By being empathetic to the needs of each remote team member and recognizing the diversity of views that employees will have on how work is done, the 4S Leader can work with the team to develop a best practice for the team to succeed.

We believe this will include a thoughtful blend of remote collaboration tools and an effort to maximize the "real time" the team can spend together. This could be weekly, monthly, or quarterly depending on the nature of the hybrid team.

Managers who work remotely may struggle even more to engage their teams. Our advice:

- Communication, accountability, and individualization are key.
- Leaders need to individualize how they support their employees.
- Maximize the "real time" you spend with employees to continually develop your personal relationship.

What new skills will need to be taught to become an effective hybrid team leader?

One thing is clear: The widespread change to remote work happened too quickly for companies to effectively train their managers. In fact, most managers were forced to learn on the fly.

In our online research, we found a variety of articles that can help you become an effective hybrid team leader. One article on www.Dialpad.com stood out with some excellent advice for hybrid leaders. On the Dialpad website, search for "Tips for Managing a Remote Team."

CHEMISTRY QUESTIONS

As our workplace becomes more global, remote, and diverse how do leaders develop teams that connect with strong diversity of thought?

Excellence in team chemistry begins at both the top and the bottom. At the top, the chief needs to embrace the idea that diversity of thought is important and needs to be intentional when adding new team members. At the bottom, all team members need to lean-in and ask that their diverse voices are heard and respected.

Intentional leaders should develop a diversity matrix when building their hybrid team. This should, at minimum, begin with a diversity of behavioral assessments, genders, ethnicities, generations (Boomers, Gen Xers, Millennials, and Zers), global and cultural background, and educational levels. As we said in Chapter 2, chemistry is hard work, but if you start with a diversity matrix and blend in team members who complement each other then you will be on the path to exceptional results.

Which of the StrengthsFinder four basic talent fields are best suited for remote work?

As you may recall, the StrengthsFinder four basic talent fields are:

1. *Striving talent (red)* – Fast paced, motivates others to action, focuses on excellence, likes a good battle
2. *Relating talent (blue)* – Even paced, open, trusting, people orientation, builds relationships, avoids confrontations
3. *Impacting talent (orange)* – Fast paced, passionate, driven, internally motivated, desires to stand out, competitive
4. *Thinking talent (green)* – Slower paced, linear, structured, practical, strategic thinking, weighs all the alternatives

We believe the "task domains" best suited for hybrid work are Striving and Thinking. The stronger "people domains" – Relating and Impacting – may find it more difficult to satisfy their desire to connect with people remotely.

Our research also indicates that different types of work have revealed higher productivity through remote work. This also supports the idea that remote work is best suited for task-driven employees and task-driven workflows.

What is the virtual/remote equivalent of "real time" – like time spent around the campfire?

Great question. The short answer is that we believe there is no virtual equivalent or replacement for quality time spent in person. Human beings have evolved massive brains for survival through rational thought and communication. It's what separates us from our fellow creatures, and our bias to be in "tribes" should be nurtured and highlighted whenever possible.

The pandemic temporarily stripped us of this evolutionary benefit, and it has been really hard on the mental health of much of the workforce. Zoom and Microsoft Teams virtual meetings have worked well to fill the communication gap, but virtual meetings do not fill the social gap. The power of campfire circles has been burned into our DNA – it's a powerful way to connect with others.

We strongly recommend your hybrid team prioritizes and maximizes face time spent together to collaborate and create. We hear from executives that they will be increasing travel budgets over the next few years, so teams can reconnect in person. We have also become big fans of "virtual happy hours" and "virtual concerts" where hybrid teams can spend time together in a casual setting. Being flexible and creative is essential to building a winning hybrid team.

COMPASS QUESTION

If hybrid team members are located in many different places, how does a leader best create a single, unified team destination?

If two team members start from different locations with the same compass heading, then they may find themselves arriving at two entirely different destinations. Regardless of different starting locations, the whole team must arrive at the identical destination. As with in-person teams, it's critical to create a shared destination by working on your compass together as a team.

After developing the team mission, winning leaders should be open to reviewing and improving the common mission on a regular cadence. Remote teams can take a fresh look at their solutions and, together, develop a new and inspiring destination for their team. When team missions are developed from within, then the team becomes more committed and engaged.

We have found that doing this important work remotely can be effective when using the proper communication tools. Once your hybrid team knows where they are going and how to get there, then keeping the destination top-of-mind is equally important.

CENTERED QUESTION

How will hybrid teams keep their balance of competition and collaboration with less interaction with other external and internal teams?

While companies have opened their offices to a hybrid work schedule, the negative effects of the pandemic may have some lasting impacts on teams.

We have been strong supporters of cross-functional teams and cross-fertilization of managers across functional areas when coaching our clients. If you are part of a special-project team, then it is in your best interest to assemble the team with a diversity matrix and make sure you have representation from all the functional areas of your company – it will make your team stronger.

I've worked as a middle manager and executive and have seen great benefits from cross-fertilization where leaders intentionally join other functional areas' team meetings. This is where the magic of collaboration begins. By witnessing other teams, a leader can learn best practices and begin the road to trust by walking in other people's shoes. Now, more than ever, begin this simple yet powerful practice to become a more centered team.

COMMUNITY QUESTIONS

If hybrid teams are spending less face time together, how do they continue to develop a strong community?

When employees are scattered everywhere, it can be particularly challenging to make all team members feel the same sense of camaraderie and belonging. It's an important consideration, because an active hybrid work community increases energy, engagement, and satisfaction and reduces stress and downtime.

We found some creative approaches in an article where members of *Forbes* Communications Council shared how they foster a strong sense of community, no matter where the team members are located. Many of these ideas address ways to make remote workers feel more connected. Visit www. Forbes.com and search for "Ways to create community in a hybrid work environment."

In our research, we were glad to see a key theme to make community building a goal and a requirement for hybrid teams. Investing in activities that help your team remember who they work with will help to build a collegial environment that will pay dividends in team engagement and productivity.

How do you maintain a culture of open and consistent communication if the hybrid team members are rarely physically together?

In our experience, and highlighted in the research from *Crucial Conversations*, challenging conversations should take place in person where both parties can gauge rapport, feel emotions, and build trust. This isn't always possible with remote teams, and we believe this has had a negative effect on building communities. We strongly encourage leaders to make "real time" together a priority and to maximize the quality of that time.

With that said, if you are a fully remote team and crucial conversations must be done through technology, then we implore you to take this advice to heart: *Do not under any circumstances make a crucial communication with a teammate through DM, texting, or email.*

We suggest reserving difficult conversations for a video call. It is ok and even preferred to use DM, texting, or email to set up the video call with some background information, so you can both prepare to hold a meaningful conversation.

And, as we said in Chapter 5, difficult conversations never get easier with time and are always better behind you than in front of you.

How do you build strong communities between people of different strengths, ethnicities, socioeconomic backgrounds, and so forth?

A strong and diverse community requires a full commitment for the entire team to be bridge builders rather than fence builders. Rather than focusing on your differences (fences), turn your focus to all that you have in common (bridges). When your team embraces inclusion, you take a significant step forward in becoming a winning, high-performing team.

CARABINER KEY POINT:

Teams that embrace inclusion will prosper. Teams that don't embrace inclusion will fail to reach their full potential.

CREATIVITY QUESTION

Will the creative energy that builds when teams are face to face be adversely affected when they are remote?

Keeping the creative juices flowing when you are not in the same room appears to be a significant challenge. Team leaders we work with express that one of the biggest challenges for creative teams is brainstorming online versus in a room together. Other vexing challenges include getting sufficient time with senior staff for key decisions, mentoring and development opportunities, and avoiding team member burnout.

In terms of collaborating when creative teams are dispersed, many practices and tools can create the "next best thing to being there." We won't mention specific collaboration tools, as new ones are coming on the market all the time. However, they are an essential foundation to keep your team connected and engaged. Whichever ones work best for you, keep in mind the following tips:

- Decide as a team which collaboration tools to use and how you will use them.
- Make sure all team members have access to and are trained to use them.
- Take time to treat all team members, including freelancers and contractors, as part of the family. Bring them into the fold by making sure they have access to all the files and resources they need to complete their work efficiently. In this competitive talent world, those contractors may be your best future hires.
- Invest and train all members on how to access, name, and share files.

One interesting prediction we are following is that creative work will become more like video games. Platforms like Virbela enable companies to build immersive 3D worlds for work, learning, and virtual events. Using these types of platforms for creative work, team members – represented by avatars – can hold a virtual brainstorming session where members can watch each other add sticky notes to a virtual whiteboard, debate the merits of an idea, and even do handstands to show support for ideas as part of a robust conversation about the ideas everyone is contributing. All the sticky notes are automatically assembled for follow-up meetings, which makes meeting summation a breeze.

This creative process enables distributed teams to collaborate in ways that are practical and fun while still being highly productive in terms of sharing and building on each other's ideas. We encourage you to keep such technologies in mind as they emerge.

Finally, we have a few tips for taking care of your fellow team members to avoid burnout:

1. Watch out for team member isolation.
2. Agree on standard work hours and honor off hours.
3. Provide some rules around on-camera meetings; if one camera is on then all cameras should be on.
4. Make meetings count with thoughtful agendas and outcomes.
5. Be on the lookout for quieter members and find space for them to contribute.
6. Sharpen your team's creative skills by collaborating on pro bono projects.
7. Pair up team members for camaraderie, mentoring, and development.

COURAGE QUESTION

If team courage requires authenticity, vulnerability, and high levels of trust, then how can hybrid teams maximize the limited time they are together?

It starts by being very intentional to maximize the precious time you do spend together. This is true whether you have budgeted communal time at two days per week or two weeks per year. Follow the six P's: "Piss-poor planning leads to piss-poor performance."

If "real time" together is at a premium, then the entire team should be involved in planning for the best outcomes. Each team member should share their expectations with the leader. It's always a good idea to engage your company's resources such as HR and meeting planners. They typically have the best relationships with off-site meeting locations and hotels. They will also have relationships with the best team-building professionals.

The ROI for maximizing the quality time spent with your employees will have a quick payback in team engagement, retention, and performance.

HYBRID TEAMS QUESTION

We should start by saying that as an outdoor leadership company we are not the best technology consultants. However, we have learned from our clients what seems to work best. When it comes to leading hybrid teams, 4S Leaders should be open, flexible, and equitable with their teams:

- Open to evolving new technologies and willing to test new ideas.
- Flexible to accommodate the needs of individual team members, as everyone's circumstances are unique.
- Equitable in the treatment of all team members, so no single person receives better treatment due to unique circumstances. Some of our clients have set equitable guidelines such as "we all meet in person, or we all meet by video." No preferential treatment.

We respect communication technologies such as Slack and Microsoft Teams, which have found the middle ground of helping hybrid teams collaborate. We also hear of technology going too far and being too intrusive. If you want to break the trust of your team, go ahead and implement mandatory online tracking or GPS tracking! Simply put, it is best to manage performance and not compliance.

SEE YOU AT THE TOP

We hope you enjoyed your climb up the 7 Summits and that, from the top, you can look out at our ever-changing world with a new, 360-degree perspective. The view from the top will give you a new understanding of your customers and competitors, so you know which mountains to climb next.

We believe the seven common traits in winning teams that we have witnessed over the past twenty years – and continue to witness – will hold true for many years to come. Humans are complicated creatures who need teams more than ever to win in our complex world. Our *7 Summits* book team wishes you all the best in your climb. We believe greatness lies within your team. Onward and upward!

7 Summits Team Assessment

	Strongly disagree	Disagree	Somewhat disagree	Somewhat agree	Agree	Strongly Agree
CHIEF						
1. Our leaders value employee growth over personal recognition.	O	O	O	O	O	O
2. Management knows my strengths and are committed to my success.	O	O	O	O	O	O
3. Our team projects are often micromanaged.	O	O	O	O	O	O
Chemistry						
4. I trust my co-workers and can share my personal challenges with them.	O	O	O	O	O	O
5. Personal agendas often get in the way of doing the right thing for the team.	O	O	O	O	O	O
6. Team members are purposely selected to represent diversity in thought.	O	O	O	O	O	O
Compass						
7. Team members give their support to team decisions that they may not fully agree with.	O	O	O	O	O	O
8. My daily work is in alignment with our mission statement.	O	O	O	O	O	O
9. Our team has a clear common purpose and a single destination.	O	O	O	O	O	O

	Strongly disagree	Disagree	Somewhat disagree	Somewhat agree	Agree	Strongly Agree
Community						
10. Team members are willing to address unpopular issues and seek timely solutions.	O	O	O	O	O	O
11. I enjoy socializing with co-workers away from work.	O	O	O	O	O	O
12. My organization volunteers its resources to the local community.	O	O	O	O	O	O
13. Team members follow through on their commitments.	O	O	O	O	O	O
Centered						
14. I am in competition with my coworkers for recognition and promotions.	O	O	O	O	O	O
15. Our team is willing to share best practices and information across the organization.	O	O	O	O	O	O
16. Team members make team results a priority over individual gains.	O	O	O	O	O	O

	Strongly disagree	Disagree	Somewhat disagree	Somewhat agree	Agree	Strongly Agree
Creativity						
17. Our leaders encourage us to take risks and try new ideas.	O	O	O	O	O	O
18. We get sidetracked by real or perceived obstacles.	O	O	O	O	O	O
19. My work group generates creative solutions by seeking the ideas from all team members.	O	O	O	O	O	O
Courage						
20. Our leaders are strong and rarely show vulnerability or admit to making mistakes.	O	O	O	O	O	O
21. Our reward and recognition system encourages risk taking.	O	O	O	O	O	O
22. Our Leaders are often on the front lines and seeking new solutions for our customers.	O	O	O	O	O	O

NEXT STEPS:

1. You can photocopy and hand out this assessment and ask your team to complete it at your next gathering. Alternatively, you and your team can take this survey online at www.ParkCityTeamworks.com. Thanks to the help of Survey Monkey, you will receive some complimentary analytics.

2. Next, we encourage you to engage the Park City Teamworks professionals in a complimentary interview by phone or video conference call.

3. We will follow up the call with an outline of priorities to facilitate your team's climb to the top.

Park City Teamworks Partial Client List

Abbott Laboratories	AbbVie	Adobe Systems
Alliance Residential	America First Credit Union	American Red Cross
Amgen	ARUP Laboratories	AstraZeneca
Autoliv	Aveda Corporation	Bayer
BD Medical	Beezer Homes USA	BioFire Diagnostics
Blackstone	Bristol Myers Squibb	BTG International Limited
Carbo Ceramics Inc.	Cargill	Coca-Cola
Dow Chemical Co.	Dow Corning	Dynastar
Dyno Nobel Inc.	eBay	eBay Motors
Edwards Lifesciences	EGR International	Eli Lilly
Ernst & Young	Extra Space Storage	FedEx
Firehouse Subs	Franklin Covey Co.	Franklin Electric
GE Capital	GE Healthcare	GE Water & Process Technologies
Genentech	General Electric	Gerber Products Company

Goodway Group	GSK plc	H&R Block
Hines Securities, Inc.	IBM	Infor
Johnson & Johnson	Joy Global	JPMorgan Chase
JW Marriott Hotels	Keen	Kellogg
Korn Ferry	KPMG	L-3 Communications Holdings
LANDesk	Land Rover	MedImmune
Merck & Co.	Meritage Homes Corporation	Microsoft Corporation
Mini Cooper	Morgan Stanley	Mountain Hardwear
Myriad Genetics	Nike	Nu Skin Enterprises
Oracle Corporation	PacifiCorp	PepsiCo
Pfizer	Phillips	Philips 66
PricewaterhouseCoopers	Proctor & Gamble	PulteGroup
Red Bull	Robert Half	Salesforce
Sanofi	Shell Oil	Simplot
Sinclair Oil Corporation	Skullcandy	Sprint Corporation
Synchrony	Sysco	Tetra Pak
Texaco	Texas Roadhouse Grill	Timberland
Toll Brothers	Tyson Foods	UBS Group
United Egg Producers	Usana Health Sciences	US Ski & Snowboard
US Translation Company	Vivint	VMI Nutrition Inc.
Wells Fargo	Western Governors University	Xerox
YEO – Young Entrepreneurs Organization	YPO – Young Presidents Organization	Zions Bank

ABOUT THE AUTHOR

JUDD EFINGER has paired a thirty-year career in sales management with running an outdoor leadership and corporate team-building company in Park City, Utah. As founder of Park City Teamworks, Judd has designed business adventures for more than 500 companies and 40,000 business leaders.

The outdoor adventures have proven to be the perfect setting to see how business teams play under stress and reveal their true nature. Back at Base Camp, debriefings help team members apply the lessons learned in their outdoor adventure to become a high-performing, winning team when they return to the office.

Previously, as vice president of sales in the water-management sector, Judd led teams as large as fifty sales reps with more than $200 million in annual revenue. In addition, he has been a contributing member of two executive leadership teams and has served on many community nonprofits as a board member. He also served two terms as president of the Park City Sunrise Rotary Club.

Judd has lived in the Wasatch Mountains of Utah since 1994 with his wife Lisa and their three children. They share a passion for mountain adventures including hiking, mountain climbing, mountain biking, and skiing. They are currently building a new home in Sun Valley, Idaho.

Judd has reached the summit of most of the highest peaks in the American West, and in 2000 he climbed three peaks (17,600 to 21,100 feet in elevation) in the Bolivian Andes to raise money for a friend he lost to leukemia.

Learn more about Judd Efinger and how he can help your team reach the top with Executive Retreats/Recharges, Sales Coaching, and Speaking at www.JuddEfinger.com.

JUDD EFINGER'S
TOP 20
FAVORITE BUSINESS BOOKS

In the last thirty years, Judd has read hundreds of business books. A few rise to the top, and he's sharing his list of favorites.

Make the commitment to being a life-long learner and teacher. Make the commitment to becoming the best business leader you can be!

START HERE:

Receive your complimentary list of Judd Efinger's Top 20 Favorite Business Books. Email your request to Elevate@JuddEfinger.com

Join the climb to the top!

Made in the USA
Middletown, DE
16 October 2022